Bless Your Heart, You Freakin' Idiot.

Southern Sayings Translated
By Tim Heaton

D1534021

Acknowledgements

This book is the product of generations of Southern families and extra help from:

Barry Aluisa,

Andi Jenea Bobo,

Sherry Eaton,

Anita C Estep,

Jonathan Jamerson,

Gigi Goss Lewis,

Rhonda Lindsay,

Allison Pace,

Dru Reynolds,

Kathy Hilliard Sanders,

Jenny F Strother,

Melody Waller,

Jim Woodrick.

Front cover is by Samuel Panko

Back cover art is from the paintings of Cameron Knight Watson

Introduction

Bless your heart!

I've heard this phrase all my life. Many Southern women use it without ever knowing they've said it. It is an interjection like "Oh for Pete's sake" or "Mother Mary and Joseph" that one hears often in the north.

The proper translation of the phrase is complex. Often it is necessary for the listener to observe visual clues given by the speaker. "Bless Your Heart" can be used to show sympathy, concern and affection; as well as pity, disapproval, or to deliver a verbal backhand. There really isn't much subterfuge as many commentators suggest.

Who initiates a topic in which is granted a "Bless your heart" is the key to the intended meaning. If the speaker makes an observation, and follows with the phrase, it usually means sympathy, concern and affection. For example:

"She likes her cocktails – bless her heart." - Would likely be sympathy.

"Bless her heart, she enjoys cocktails." - Shows concern, or affection.

On the other hand, if "Bless your heart" follows a statement by another person, the phrase is usually conveying pity, disapproval, or a verbal backhand. For example:

Northerner: "I don't understand the fuss about college football."
Southerner: "Well, bless your heart" - This means: I regret your lack of manners.

Northerner: "Why is everyone dressed up for tailgating?"
Southerner: "Why, bless your heart." This means: You should be easy to replace by the next game.

And finally….

Northerner: "Southern food is just awful; I can't find a good pizza anywhere."
Southerner: "Why, bless your heart. I'll help you pack." This means: You are a freakin' idiot.

How to Enjoy This Book.

It is not be hurried through; take your time and enjoy. This collection of Southernisms is one of the largest available. Every saying is categorized into fifty topic chapters from "Angry" to "Yes"; and each of those categories has a short, funny yarn about that topic. However, what makes this book unique is that each saying is annotated with alternative sayings, explanations, facts, and similar quotes from famous people. I hope you enjoy "Bless Your Heart, You freakin' Idiot." Use the sayings, and remember:

"Wise sayings often fall on barren ground, but a kind word is never thrown away."
Arthur Helps 1813-1875

Table of Contents

How Much? By the skin of my teeth.

Impoverished: Too poor to paint, too proud to whitewash.

Insults: Can't never could.

Intoxicated: Drunker than a bicycle.

Luck: Both Kinds.

Meals: So good you'll want to slap granny.

Momma Said: Don't be ugly.

Nervous: Like a cat on a hot tin roof.

No: I'd rather sandpaper a bobcat's ass in a phone booth.

Odors: It could knock a buzzard off a gut wagon.

Plumpish: It takes two dogs to bark at her.

Proverbs: A gallant retreat is better than a bad stand.

Scrawny: They look poorly.

Shiftless: As useful as tits on a tricycle.

Skinflints: He knows every dollar by first name.

Speed – Faster: than a frog shot out of a barn.

Speed – Slower: than a herd of turtles racing in peanut butter.

Surprised: Knock me over with a feather duster.

Threats: You're going to Hell on a scholarship.

Time: You can't hurry up good times by waiting for them.

Tough: He's scared of nothing but spiders and dry counties

Trifling: It's like two mules fighting over a turnip.

Troublesome: Harder to catch than my wife's boyfriend.

Villains: More slippery than a pocketful of pudding.

Wealthy: Shitting in tall cotton.

Weary: Still kickin', but not high, still floppin', but can't fly.

Weather: The Devil's beatin' his wife with a frying pan.

Yes: Good Lord willing and the creek don't rise.

Prologue

About the Author

Angry: Ill as a hornet.

Getting a Southerner to show anger is simply a matter of breaking through the boundary of good manners to get to the zone where duels were once fought. Politics and religion are poor topics of discussion of course. All the same, outsiders are often surprised to learn that Southerners have a "live and let live" philosophy. Uneducated observations on the culture of the South may get you a stern look. However, if you're trying to get under a Southerners' skin, the fastest way is to insult one's family or the flag. Here are the sayings you might hear as you get closer to the dueling zone.

About to have a dying duck fit!
☺Note: "Dying Duck Fit" is a DEFCON level above a "Duck Fit"

Dills my pickle!
☺Note: In the Delta region of Mississippi, Kool-Aid pickles have become popular. The recipe is simple: take some dill pickles, cut them in half, and then soak them in super strong Kool-Aid for a week.

Don't let your bulldog mouth overload your hummingbird ass.
☺"One of the most important things, especially when you're leaving school, is to realize you're going to be dealing with a lot of idiots. And a lot of those idiots are in charge of things, so if you're in an interview and you really want to tell the person off, don't do it."
Lewis Black

Don't pee down my back and tell me it's raining!
☺Rather than: I'll kick your ass so hard you'll have to unbutton your collar to shit.

Don't rush on my account!
☺ Rather than: Let's go! - While we're young!

Fit to be tied!
☺ Rather than: I am barking mad.

Fly off the handle.
☺Note: This is an original American phrase and it alludes to the uncontrolled way a loose axe-head flies off from its handle.

Go sit in the truck!
☺Meaning: Shut up and leave me be.

He's got his tail up.
☺Meaning: His blood is up.

He's madder than a puffed toad.
☺Fact: Toads don't drink water, they absorb it through their skin.

I could chew up nails and spit out a barbed wire fence.
☺Fact: In 1860, Frenchman Leonce Eugene Grassin-Baledans patented Barbed Wire: twisted strands of sheet metal with projecting points as a "fence protector."

I have three speeds: on, off, and don't push your luck.
☺Meaning: Don't test my patience because if I lose my patience you will become a patient.

I was as mad as a three-legged dog trying to bury a turd on an icy pond.
☺Fact: A scientific study revealed that dogs adapt their excremental habits to align with the planet's geomagnetic field.

I'll kill you and swear you died.
☺ Rather than: I can go from zero to psycho in one text message flat.

I'll knock your teeth so far down your throat you'll spit 'em out in single file.
☺Also: I'll hit you so hard you'll be shitting teeth.

I'm about to have a hissy fit.

☺Note: The DEFCON stages are "hissy fit", "duck fit", "hissy fit with a tail on it", and finally "dying duck fit" – at which time it is too late to make amends.

I'm mad enough to drown puppies.

☺Note: Don't get that angry, Pet Finder has a nationwide network of 12,462 adoption groups.

I'm so mad I could spit!

☺Fact: Each justice of the Supreme Court of the United States continues to be provided with a personal cuspidor.

I'm going to do it even if it hair-lips the world (or Governor, Pope or President.)

☺ Meaning: I'm determined to get it done.

I'm going to jerk you bald!

☺Fact: The average person's scalp has up to 150,000 hair follicles.

I'm going to skin you alive!

☺Fact: Burn victims with over 90% coverage have been saved.

I'm ill as a hornet!

☺Fact: Hornets aren't native to North America, they introduced here by accident.

I'm so mad I could just fall out of my pants.

☺ Rather than: You think I'm cute when I'm mad? I'm about to be freakin' gorgeous.

If you don't stop, I'll tear your arm off and beat you to death with the bloody stump.

☺Rather than: Talk to the hand. If you have questions, consult my middle finger.

Mad as a box of frogs.

☺ Rather than: Mad as a raging bull.

Mad as a mule chewing on bumblebees.
☺Fact: A mule is the result of the mating of a male donkey (jack) and a female horse (mare) to produce a hybrid.

Madder than a bobcat caught in a piss fire.
☺Fact: To start a fire, fill a plastic bag with urine, then use it as a magnifying glass to burn tinder.

Madder than a boiled owl.
☺"Push my buttons, and I'll push you off a bridge."   Karen Quan

Madder than a Wampus Cat in a rainstorm.
☺Note: A "Wampus Cat" is a mythical half-woman, half-cat, from Cherokee mythology.

Madder than a wet settin' hen.
☺Note: Farmers used to dunk hens in cold water to break them out of broodiness. "Broodiness" is the tendency for hens to collect a clutch of eggs to hatch.

Madder than a pack of wild dogs on a three legged cat.
☺Fact: To a cat, a wagging tail is a sign of anger or displeasure.

Madder than the snake that married the garden hose!
☺Fact: Rat Snakes do look like black garden hoses and kill their prey by constriction.

Makes my butt want to grind corn.
☺ Rather than: I actually don't need to control my anger. Everyone around me needs to control their habit of pissing me off.

Meaner than a wet panther.
☺Fact: The Florida Panther needs 200 square miles in habitat to survive.

Panties are in a wad.
☺ For Aussies and Brits, "Knickers in a twist."

She's in a horn-tossing mood.
☺Fact: Although many Western riders will never rope a cow, the western saddle still features a horn to do it with.

Sis on you pister, you ain't so muckin' fuch!
☺Note: Southerners love to swap letters on curse words. "Piss on you mister, you ain't so fucking much!"

Time to paint your butt white and run with the antelope.
☺ Rather than: I'm going to rip off your head and pee down your throat.

Stuck in my craw like hair on a biscuit.
☺"The world needs more anger. The world often continues to allow evil because it isn't angry enough."   Bede Jarrett

You are so full of shit your eyes are brown.
☺ Rather than: I'll rip out your eyes and piss on your brain.

You better give your heart to Jesus, because your butt is mine.
☺ Rather than: I don't have a license to kill. I do, however, have a learner's permit.

You're going to ruffle feathers.
☺Fact: When angered, birds often ruffle their feathers so that they look larger.

Blue: Sucking hind teat.

The source of the word "blue" for "sad" is unknown, but it is a figure of speech common in cultures around the world. Southern sayings for "blue" are mostly related to farming, and the figures on farming as a family occupation are sobering indeed.

While food prices have gone up substantially in supermarkets, the wages farmers are paid have been left out of the equation. "It has been estimated that living expenses for the average farm family exceed $47,000 per year," an Environmental Protection Agency report stated. "Clearly, many farms that meet the U.S. Census' definition would not produce sufficient income to meet farm family living expenses. In fact, less than 1 in 4 of the farms in this country produce gross revenues in excess of $50,000."

Enjoy these sayings while you can. I don't think ConAgra will be adding to them.

I can't win for losing.
☺Meaning: Things would be going great - if they weren't going so badly.

I feel like a banjo. Everybody's picking on me.
☺Fact: The banjo was brought to America by West African slaves in the 17th Century.

I feel like the last pea at pea-time.
☺Note: The last pea would be lonely in a field of empty vines.

I feel like the red headed step child.
☺Note: At one time red hair was considered to be a sign of infidelity.

I feel lower than a bow-legged caterpillar.
☺Fact: The Monarch caterpillar is toxic, so pass on them as a pizza topping.

If momma ain't happy, ain't nobody happy.
☺Note: An obvious observation, but a saying that should be on the tip of your tongue nonetheless.

Lower than a snake's belly in a wagon rut.
☺Meaning: That one is sad; or it could be used to describe a villain.

Lower than an ankle bracelet on a flat-footed pygmy.
☺Rather than: Lower than whale shit.

Messed up like a kite in a hail storm!
☺Note: That's messed up. Imagine what a hail-assaulted kite would look like?

Sad as cucumber.
☺Fact: The skin of a cucumber will erase ink from paper.

Sucking hind teat.
☺Fact: The teat farthest from the front is less conveniently positioned and produces less milk.

Swinging my legs from a dime.
☺Note: A dime is very thin and doesn't allow for much leg-swinging.

Busy: Busier than a cat burying shit on a marble floor.

Mr. Blair's barn was a kid's dream. It was a rotating museum of things not quite old enough to be valuable, and not quite new enough to be useful. One visit the barn would be filled with old railroad lanterns. Next time, those would be gone and replaced by weather vanes. Those would be replaced in turn by antique farm implements. If he found a good deal on paint and canvas, he painted. When he found a pile of unwanted wood, he built birdhouses. Once he had a stage coach in his barn, then fire engine, then a mahogany motor boat. Sometime around his 80th birthday, the boat was replaced by the skeleton of a light airplane. I knew he was in the Navy, but I didn't know he flew. No, he said. I'm not going to fly it anywhere. I'm building it to keep young.

If Mr. Blair was really busy, here are the ways he said it.

As busy as a church fan in dog days.
☺Fact: Country churches often passed out fans during the dog days of summer.

Busier than a 2-dollar whore on nickel night.
☺Rather than: Busier than a cat covering up shit on a concrete floor.

Busier than a blind dog in a meat house.
☺Rather than: Busy as a bee.

Busier than a blind man at a striptease!
☺Rather than: Busy as a one-armed paperhanger

Busier than a cat burying shit on a marble floor.
☺Rather than: Busy as Grand Central Station

Busier than a moth in a mitten!
☺Rather than: I'm busier than a mosquito at a nudist colony.

Busier than a one-armed monkey with two peckers.

☺Also: Busy as a cat on a hot tin roof

Busier than a one-armed paper hanger with jock itch.
☺Rather than: Busy as a fish peddler in Lent

Busier than a one-legged man in a butt kicking contest.
☺Also: Busy as popcorn on a skillet

Busier than a set of jumper cables at a Mexican funeral.
☺"Life is what happens while you are busy making other plans."
John Lennon

Busier than ants at a picnic.
☺"Beware the barrenness of a busy life."   Socrates

Busy as a stump-tailed cow in fly season.
☺"You can really only enjoy life when you're extremely busy."
Josephine de La Baume

I don't have time to cuss the cat.
☺"Get busy living, or get busy dying."   Stephen King

I got more things to do than a dog with fleas.
☺Fact: Add 1 teaspoon of white distilled vinegar to 1 quart of your
dog's drinking water to deter fleas.

I'm as busy as a farmer with one hoe and two rattlesnakes.
☺"When you are asked if you can do a job, tell 'em, 'Certainly I
can!' Then get busy and find out how to do it."   Theodore Roosevelt

I'm up to my ass in alligators.
☺"When you are up to your ass in alligators it's difficult to
remember that your initial objective was to drain the swamp."
Ronald Reagan.

I'm busier than a borrowed mule.
☺Note: Since the mule is on lend for limited time, most folks would

use it as much as possible while they had it.

<u>I'm running around like a chicken with its head cut off.</u>
☺Fact: After decapitation, some animals will run (or swim) because the neural network in the spinal cord is pre-programmed to direct the muscles in frequently used movement.

Capable: Smart as a tree full of owls.

"It is not the critic who counts; not the man who points out how the strong man stumbles, or where the doer of deeds could have done them better. The credit belongs to the man who is actually in the arena, whose face is marred by dust and sweat and blood; who strives valiantly; who errs, who comes short again and again, because there is no effort without error and shortcoming; but who does actually strive to do the deeds; who knows great enthusiasms, the great devotions; who spends himself in a worthy cause; who at the best knows in the end the triumph of high achievement, and who at the worst, if he fails, at least fails while daring greatly, so that his place shall never be with those cold and timid souls who neither know victory nor defeat." Theodore Roosevelt

Teddy's mother, Martha Stewart "Mittie" Bulloch, was not just a Southern Belle, but the model Margaret Mitchell used for Scarlett O'Hara in Gone With the Wind." Teddy might have heard these Southernisms from his mother.

A can of corn and a pop fly.
☺Meaning: Easy, as they are both easy to master.

Ain't no hill for a climber.
☺Meaning: Not a big deal for someone with experience.

Ain't no thang but a chicken wang (wing).
☺Rather than: It's not a big deal.

Easier than falling off a greasy log.
☺Rather than: Like shooting fish in a barrel.

Handier than a shirt pocket.
☺Fact: This saying, and the pocket itself, is French in origin.

He could talk the dogs off a meat truck.
☺Rather than: He could charm wallpaper off a wall.

I wouldn't trade her for a farm in Georgia.
☺Fact: Georgia is the number one producer of pecans in the world.
Note: Pecan is pronounced "puh-kahn," not "pee-can." A pee-can is a bed-pan.

I'm just a country boy.
☺Meaning: They aren't just a country boy, so don't play poker with one.

If she says her hen dips snuff, you can look under the wing for a can.
☺Meaning: Because I said so. Fact: The phrase has long been popular in African-American vernacular. In 1929, Blind Willie McTell's song "Kind Mama" and Louis Armstrong used the full phrase in their songs.

No flies on them.
☺Meaning: "Alive" and someone who is intelligent and able to think quickly

She could sell salt to a snail.
☺Also: She could sell Raid to a bug

Smart as a tree full of owls.
☺Fact: Most species of owls can't be trained at all, they only look smart because of the size of their eyes.

Smart as a whip.
☺Fact: If you've even been tagged by a whip, it smarts

Useful as a prefabricated post hole.
☺Fact: In tough ground, a power auger may not be enough. Be nice to have a prefab post hole wouldn't it?

Charming: She's finer than frog hair split eight ways!

My sons, who were raised in New Jersey, are at the age where they're asking for tips on meeting Southern girls – a variety of female worth looking into. My advice is usually, "Why don't you start with something easier, like getting accepted to Harvard." Still, I can't help but admire their ambition — they've apparently done some reconnoiter during tailgates at the Ole Miss Grove. Here are some of the sayings you will need to know.

Cute as a bug's ear.
☺Fact: 'Cute' was a synonym for 'acute' in the 18th century England. The term crossed the Atlantic and in 1848 the US romantic poet James Russell Lowell penned the phrase: "Aint it cute to see a Yankee Take sech everlastin' pains? "Cute as a bug's ear" was first penned in the Charleston Sunday News, June 1891.

Cuter than pig nipples.
☺Fact: The person calling herself Jasmine Tridevil, claimed to have a breast added (making it three), but three breasts do occur naturally in humans - more often in men than women.

Prettier than a speckled pup under a wagon with his tongue hanging out.
☺"I was about half in love with her by the time we sat down. That's the thing about girls. Every time they do something pretty... you fall half in love with them, and then you never know where the hell you are." J. D. Salinger

Pretty as a mess of fried catfish.
☺Fact: "Mess" is Southern for a "batch." This would translate to: Pretty as a "batch" of fried catfish.

Pretty as a spotted horse in a daisy pasture.
☺"Learn how to fake a smile that doesn't look fake." Marilyn Monroe

She had a butt like a forty-dollar mule. (Or government mule)
☺Fact: Before the tractor, farmers used mules to plow, and they only wanted mules with muscular hind quarters.

She has legs to lunch box!
☺Fact: Christie Brinkley, Kate Moss, Twiggy and Naomi Campbell are all famed for their impressive stems.

She's hot as a 2 dollar pistol.
☺Fact: From a George Jones song. A cheap pistol, due to thinner steel in the barrel, gets hot quickly when firing

She's finer than frog hair split eight ways!
☺Rather than: I would drink her daddy's bath water.

She's pretty as a speckled pup.
☺"Any man who can drive safely while kissing a pretty girl is simply not giving the kiss the attention it deserves." Albert Einstein

As full of wind as a corn-eating horse.
☺Fact: The gastrointestinal system of a horse measures, on average, 100 feet and holds approximately 48 gallons of fecal matter.

Chatty: If bullshit were music, he'd have a brass band.

Communication Addiction Disorder or "Talk-aholism", affects 300 million people; or more accurately - all the rest of humanity. In a strange twist, 300 million is also the number of the most active Twitter accounts. Beware, the difference between a spoken phrase and one sent out to social media is that it is there FOREVER.

This example compliments of dumbesttweets.com: "On my way to London!! This should be exciting!!! I won't miss the lights on the Eiffel Tower this time."

Here are several expressions used to describe Communication Addiction Disorder, ie chatty.

Ask him the time and he'll tell you how to build a watch.
☺Fact: Depending on the complexity of the movement, it can take 18 months to build a timepiece like the TOURBOGRAPH "Pour le Mérite".

Could lick a skillet in the kitchen from the front porch.
☺Fact: A shotgun shack had the kitchen in back of the house, so that to reach it would take a tongue of about 30 feet – that's chatty.

Full of gas with nowhere to go.
☺Fact: The most popular basket balloons can carry up to 3-5 people and has 99,000 cubic ft. of gas.

Got tongue enough for ten rows of teeth.
☺Fact: Even sharks typically have two or three rows of mature teeth.

He blew in on his own wind.
☺"It's a mistake to think that the blow-hards who call in speak for the nation." Donella Meadows

He could talk the gate off its hinges.
☺"The trouble with her is that she lacks the power of conversation

but not the power of speech." George Bernard Shaw

He could talk the hide off a cow.
☺"If talk is cheap, then being silent is expensive. And many people it seems, can't afford to buy into it." Anthony Liccione

He could talk the legs off a chair.
☺"When an illiterate gets angry, you'll get to understand that calmness is probably a sign of education." Michael Bassey Johnson

He shoots off his mouth so much he must eat bullets for breakfast.
☺Fact: Steven Woodmore holds the record for being able to articulate 637 words per minute, a speed four times faster than the average person.

He will talk your ear off.
☺"The trouble with her is that she lacks the power of conversation but not the power of speech." George Bernard Shaw"

He'd drive a wooden Indian crazy.
☺Fact: As early as the 17th century, European tobacconists used figures of American Indians to advertise their shops.

He's a manure salesman with a mouthful of samples.
☺"They think they can make fuel from horse manure - now, I don't know if your car will be able to get 30 miles to the gallon, but it's sure gonna put a stop to siphoning. Billie Holiday

He'll tell you how the cow ate the cabbage.
☺"Not every person that speaks less than you do is more ignorant than you are." Mokokoma Mokhonoana

He's a live dictionary.
☺"The chief drawback with men is that they are too talkative." Marilyn Monroe

He's got a ten-gallon mouth.

☺"Those who say don't know, those who know don't say." Michael Lewis

Her mouth is going like a bell clapping out of a goose's ass.
☺"Those that know ain't telling me…or you." Tim Heaton

Her mouth runs like a boarding house toilet.
☺Note: A running toilet can waste 80,000 gallons of water a month.

His tongue wags at both ends.
☺"But always, it has been truly said, the savage is talkative about his mythology and taciturn about his religion." G.K. Chesterton

If bullshit were music, he'd have a brass band!
☺"Knowledge is talkative, refuses to shut up..Wisdom is so subtle, refuses to be invisible." Abha Maryada Banerjee,

She beats her own gums to death.
☺Rather than: She could talk the legs off an iron pot.

She could talk a coon right out of a tree.
☺Rather than: She talk the hind leg off a donkey.

She speaks ten words a second - with gusts to fifty.
☺"The trouble with her is that she lacks the power of conversation but not the power of speech." George Bernard Shaw

So windy he could blow up an onion sack.
☺Fact: In Blue Hill, Nebraska, it is illegal for a woman "wearing a hat that would scare a timid person" to eat onions in public.

They were vaccinated with a Victrola.
☺Fact: Tungsten was the common material for photograph needles, but for audiophiles of the period, soft wood-like fiber needles were also available for the Victrola. Although gave great sound, they dulled very quickly and had to be replaced or re-sharpened.

<u>Windy as a sack full of farts.</u>
☺Fact: According to NASA, human flatus is about 7% methane, but (pun intended) also includes nitrogen, CO_2, oxygen, and a large amount of Hydrogen.

Complaints: Don't Get Your Panties in a Wad.

Kids love to complain. Around my house these complaints center on: homework (too much), pizza (too little), bed time (too early). If you feel as if your head is trapped in a bowl of talkative gnats, these sayings will help you through anything. Well, anything short of a trip to Disney – for that medication and professional help may be needed.

Don't anything hurt a duck but his bill.
☺Meaning: Be quiet. A duck can only give up its location if it quacks.

Don't get your bowels in an uproar, your kidneys in a downpour and your liver in a jar.
☺Meaning: Just relax please.

Don't get your panties in a wad.
☺Note: What to say if the dance recital is snowed out.

Every path has a few puddles.
☺Meaning: A reminder that life is not going to be free of challenges.

If a bullfrog had wings, he wouldn't bump his ass when he jumped.
☺Rather than: If, "ifs" and "ands" were pots and pans, there would be no need for tinkers.

If ifs and buts were candy and nuts, everyday would be Christmas.
☺Note: It is used to express the fact someone has used "if" and "but" too many times.

If wishes were horses, then beggars would ride.
☺Note: An English language proverb and nursery rhyme first published in the 16th century.

If your aunt had nuts she'd be your uncle.

☺Meaning: It's useless to wish and that better results will be achieved through action

It's not what it's worth; it's what it'll bring.
☺Note: Words you're likely to hear if you're pawning your daddy's watch.

Most of the stuff people worry about ain't never gonna happen.
☺Rather than: Don't sweat the small stuff- and it's all small stuff.

Not ever on a galloping horse.
☺Meaning: No one will notice, they will be watching something else, i.e. the horse.

She could start an argument in an empty house.
☺Note: Take special note of this advice during family gatherings.

They would argue with a stoplight. (Or neon sign)
☺Meaning: Some people need the last word – even with inanimate objects

They would yank out a stop-sign to argue with the hole.
☺Note: This is an upgrade from "arguing with a stop sign" for sure.

The only thing fair in the world is the hair on a Norwegian albino's butt.
☺Meaning: That if you think life is unfair, it's because you may not understand the rules.

There's not much difference between a Hornet and a Yellow Jacket if they're in your clothes.
☺Meaning: The problem is you're being stung - by whom doesn't much matter.

Wish in one hand and shit in the other and see which one fills up first.
☺Rather than: If wishes were fishes we all wouldn't starve.

Confused: I didn't know whether to scratch my watch or wind my butt.

A confused mind is an open mind. Quotes from Albert Einstein abound on this topic, but George Saunders is also worth knowing.

"Don't be afraid to be confused. Try to remain permanently confused. Anything is possible. Stay open, forever, so open it hurts, and then open up some more, until the day you die, world without end, amen."

When you're open to the possibilities, you may hear several of these sayings.

A cat always blinks when hit on the head with a sledgehammer.
☺Rather than: Curiosity killed the cat.

As lost as Hogan's goat.
☺Fact: "Hogan's Goat" is a 1965 play by William Alfred about a mayoral race. A "goat" in the terminology of the era was a kept man.

Confused as a fart in a fan factory.
☺Note: Fine fan factories frequently test fans. If the factory fabricates football fans, farts would be requisite features.

He was like a blind dog in a meat house.
☺"I'm not confused. I'm just well mixed."   Robert Frost

He was so confused he didn't know his ass from his elbow.
☺"Right is right, and wrong is wrong, and when people start getting it confused that means they need to sit down with some real people."
Chuck D

He's a tree high squirrel.
☺Note: Rational squirrels remain in the middle of a tree to maximize cover from birds of prey.

He's more confused than a turtle on the center stripe.
☺"Always try hard not to lose yourself the moment you lose yourself, 'cos you'll find it very difficult to find yourself." Freddie Stanley

I didn't know whether to scratch my watch or wind my butt.
☺"All you have to do is say something nobody understands and they'll do practically anything you want them to." J.D. Salinger

I didn't know if I should shit and go blind or fart and close one eye.
☺"Like a chef's salad, with good things and bad things chopped and mixed together in a vinaigrette of confusion and conflict." Lemony Snicket

I don't know if I found my rope or lost my cow.
☺"It's funny. All you have to do is say something nobody understands and they'll do practically anything you want them to." J.D. Salinger, The Catcher in the Rye

I felt like a monkey trying to do a math problem.
☺"I am both happy and sad at the same time, and I'm still trying to figure out how that could be." Stephen Chbosky

Like a bagel in a bucket of grits.
☺"The most confused we ever get is when we're trying to convince our heads of something our heart knows is a lie." Karen Marie Moning

Like a fart in a skillet.
☺"Never confuse movement with action." Ernest Hemingway

Like a monkey humping a football.
☺"There is no confusion like the confusion of a simple mind." F. Scott Fitzgerald

Like an Amish electrician.
☺"Before I came here I was confused about this subject. Having

listened to your lecture I am still confused. But on a higher level."
Enrico Fermi

Lost as last year's Easter egg.
☺"May the forces of evil become confused on the way to your house." George Carlin

Lost ball in high weeds.
☺"I had nothing to offer anybody except my own confusion." Jack Kerouac

My tongue got in front of my eyetooth and I couldn't see what I was saying.
☺Note: An "eyetooth" is a canine in the upper jaw. This means tongue-tied as well.

Running around like a chicken with its head cut off.
☺"I can't be running back and forth forever between grief and high delight." J.D. Salinger

Courtship: Give me some sugar.

Northern women get a free pass with regard to dating Southern men. However, Northern men will need a little extra guidance for Southern Belles. There are a lot of dos, but only two don'ts that you will not recover from: 1) Save your Jeff Foxworthy jokes for the Jersey shore. Southern isn't Redneck. And 2) Do not attempt a Southern accent, you'll sound like an idiot.

Southern women are just like the other women of the 19th Century. Here is a short list of the dos:

- Always open doors.

- Always offer to pay.

- Always help a lady with her chair.

- Always stand when she enters a room, or gets up to leave a room.

- Always remember that behind that sweet façade is a young lady that can field dress a deer, be nice.

Here are the Southern sayings you need to know in regard to courtship.

Ashes to ashes and dust to dust, if it wasn't for women our peckers would rust.
☺"Save a boyfriend for a rainy day - and another, in case it doesn't rain." Mae West

Bait the cow to catch the calf.
☺Meaning: Be nice to your significant others' mothers.

Candy is dandy but liquor is quicker.
☺"I wish you'd keep my hands to yourself." Grouch Marx

Don't blame the cow when the milk gets sour.
☺"Statistically speaking, there is a 65 percent chance that the love of

your life is having an affair. Be very suspicious."   Scott Dikkers

Don't he think he's cock o' the hen-house?
☺Also: Sad is the house where the hen crows and the rooster is silent!

Even a dog knows the difference between being stumbled over and kicked.
☺"Every time you try to flirt with her, a puppy dies."   Maureen Johnson

Give me some sugar.
☺Meaning: Give me a kiss

Go for the ugly early and you'll never go home alone.
☺Rather than: Women sometimes make fools of men, but most guys are the do-it-yourself type.

He is welcome to eat Ritz crackers in my bed anytime.
☺"Some people think having large breasts makes a woman stupid. Actually, it's quite the opposite: a woman having large breasts makes men stupid"   Rita Rudner

Her backside looks like two Indian boys fighting under a blanket.
☺Note: Also quotes in Steel Magnolias, Clairee Belcher: "Looks like two pigs fightin' under a blanket."

Hornier than a two-peckered billy goat.
☺"Whenever I see a gorgeous woman, I think, Who is that tall drink of water, and how come I'm suddenly thirsty."   Jarod Kintz

I am sugar in your hand.
☺"Flirting is a woman's trade, one must keep in practice."
Charlotte Brontë

I couldn't get nailed in a wood workshop.
☺Rather than: I'm not unlucky at love, just incredibly lucky with

celibacy.

I didn't take her to raise.
☺Meaning: She is not my responsibility.

I'd fight tigers in the dark with a switch for him.
☺Fact: Studies find that women go for more masculine-looking men when they're ovulating, ie: strong-jawed faces, muscular bodies, dominant behaviors, deep voices and tallness.

I'd jump on that like a duck on a June-bug.
☺Rather than: I think sex is better than logic, but I can't prove it.

I've got church in the morning.
☺Meaning: You better hurry. Irish foreplay: "Brace yourself Brigette.

If I had that swing on my back porch I'd ride it every night.
☺"Too much of a good thing can be wonderful." Mae West

If it has tires or testicles, it's gonna give you trouble.
☺Men have two emotions: Hungry and Horny. If you see him without an erection, make him a sandwich.

If promises were persimmons, possums could eat good at her place.
☺Note: In Pete Seeger's song "Raccoon's got a bushy tail," possum hunts ended at the foot of a persimmon tree.

If you can sleep with 'em, I can eat with 'em!
☺Note: You may be tempted to have a few cocktails to cope with someone you don't prefer, but research shows that drinking alcohol makes you more likely to wake during the night. Get ready to chew that arm off.

Alimony is like putting gas in a car that you've already wrecked.
☺"Paying alimony is like feeding hay to a dead horse." Groucho Marx

Marriage is an expensive way for a man to get free laundry.
☺Rather than: Don't get married. Find a woman you hate and give her a house.

Marry in haste, repent in leisure.
☺"Flirting with madness was one thing; when madness started flirting back, it was time to call the whole thing off." Rohinton Mistry

Rooster one day, a feather duster the next.
☺"Times go by turns, and chances change by course, from foul to fair, from better happy to worse." Robert Southwell

She got her trotting harness on.
☺Meaning: She is dressed to be noticed. Note: Since its humble beginnings as a farmers' sport, trotting has become an international favorite. Tracks devoted to harness races exclusively appeared all over the world.

She had a voice that would chip paint.
☺"I require three things in a man: he must be handsome, ruthless, and stupid." Dorothy Parker

She was all over that like a bad rash on a big ass.
☺"I generally avoid temptation unless I can't resist it." Mae West

She was batting her eyes like a toad in a hail storm.
☺"I hope to start enjoying flirting again when I'm 70, like my mother did." Felicity Kendal

She is anyone's dog that will hunt with her.
☺"When I'm good, I'm very good. But when I'm bad I'm better." Mae West

She's like a booger that you can't thump off.
☺"Sometimes I feel my whole life has been one big rejection."

Marilyn Monroe

She's limber as a dishrag.
☺"Cultivate your curves - they may be dangerous but they won't be avoided." Mae West

She's not too pretty for nice, but great for good.
☺The more men as a group, disagree about a woman's looks, the more they end up liking her.

Sure as the vine twines 'round the stump, you are my darlin' sugar lump.
☺"I'm worth more dead than alive. Don't cry for me after I'm gone; cry for me now." Marlene Dietrich

That man has got a thumping gizzard for a heart.
☺Note: A "gizzard" is a bird's muscular alimentary canal that has usually thick muscular walls and a tough horny lining for grinding food.

That's a hard dog to keep on the porch.
☺"A hard man is good to find." Mae West

The more you cry, the less you have to piss.
☺"Crying is cleansing. There's a reason for tears, happiness or sadness." Dionne Warwick

Trouble with a milk cow is she won't stay milked.
☺A dairy cow can produce about 2,300 gallons of milk a year.

Wasn't nothin' between him and the Lord but a smile.
☺"If you can make a girl laugh, you can make her do anything." Marilyn Monroe

Well, ain't he just the tom-cat's kitten?
☺"All my life I've been flirting. I'm no different. I still carry on the same way." Guy Laliberte

What's good for the goose is good for the gander.
☺"We made eyes at each other, and then we made love. We also made other things too, like meatloaf."   Jarod Kintz

Why buy the cow if you get the milk for free.
☺"A gentleman is simply a patient wolf."   Lana Turner

Women have to be more beautiful than smart, because men see better than they think.
☺"It isn't what I do, but how I do it. It isn't what I say, but how I say it, and how I look when I do it and say it."   Mae West

You can catch more bees with honey.
☺"Why slap them on the wrist with feather when you can belt them over the head with a sledgehammer."   Katharine Hepburn

You can't ride two horses with one ass.
☺Meaning: One relationship at a time.

You could give her Heaven and Earth - she'd still want a pea patch in Hell.
☺"Sometimes I wonder if men and women really suit each other. Perhaps they should live next door and just visit now and then."
Katharine Hepburn

Crazy: You don't have to hang from a tree to be a nut.

"This is the South and we're proud of our crazy people. We don't hide them up in the attic, we bring them right down to the living room to show them off. No one in the South ever asks if you have crazy people in your family, they just ask what side they're on."
Dixie Carter

Southerners love eccentrics. William Faulkner walked about town in his Royal Air Corps uniform. In Memphis, Robert Hodges, better known as Prince Mongo, is often seen around town with a long wig, aviation goggles, and a rubber chicken attached to his jacket.

Not surprisingly then, Southerners have many phrases to describe beloved characters.

As crazy as a betsy bug.
☺Note: The "bessie" or "betsy bug," is also known as the "horn beetle", "patent-leather beetle" and "pinch bug." They fly erratically and make lots of noise, and seem...well...crazy.

As crazy as an outhouse rat.
☺Meaning: Only the crazy rats would live in an outhouse.

Crazier than a dog in a hubcap factory.
☺Crazy as a dog in a cat factory.

Crazier than a shit-house fly.
☺Meaning: Aggressive and crazy.

Crazy as a run-over cat.
☺ Fact: A disorder known as Hyperesthesia is a condition that can make a cat react as they're having a can nip fit. This disease can actually cause the skin along the spine of your cat to ripple.

Crazy as a shot at rat.
☺Note: Rat-shot is very small lead shot cartridge (typically #12 shot)

for use in rifled firearms.

Crazy as a soup sandwich.
☺Note: If you don't think that's crazy, make one and try to eat it.

Crazy as a sprayed cockroach.
☺Meaning: Running around like a chicken with it's head cut off.

He's about half a bubble off plumb.
☺Fact: The "plumb bob" has been used since at least ancient Egypt to ensure that buildings are "plumb", or vertical.

He's nuttier than a squirrel turd.
☺Fact: Never seen a squirrel turd? You probably won't. Squirrels can defecate on the run and the skat is the size of a grain of rice.

He's two bricks short of a load.
☺Also: A beer short of a six-pack. Or a few logs short of a cord. Or a few sandwiches short of a picnic. Or one fry short of a Happy Meal. Or three pickles shy of a quart.

He's lost his vertical hold.
☺Rather than: Crazy as a cat in catnip.

Head full of stump water.
☺Note: In The Adventures of Tom Sawyer, Tom Sawyer proposes "stump-water" or spunk-water as a remedy for warts.

Kangaroos are loose in the top paddock.
☺"Eccentric: A man too rich to be called crazy." Anonymous

Loopy as a cross-eyed cowboy.
☺"Honesty is the best policy, but insanity is a better defense."
Steve Landesberg

Nuttier than a five-pound fruitcake.
☺Russell Baker claims to be in possession of a fruitcake that a

relative baked in 1794 as a Christmas gift for George Washington. (He allegedly sent it back.) Baker and his relatives gather each year to savor a tiny morsel of the fruitcake.

Nuttier than a port-a-potty at a peanut festival.
☺Fact: The National Peanut Festival is largest peanut festival, held each fall in Dothan, Alabama.

Only got one oar in the water.
☺Note: The expression dates back to the sixteenth century and has turned up in all sorts of different formulations down the centuries.

She's got a bee in her bonnet.
☺Note: This saying has been around since the late 1790s. It also means to be "obsessed."

Slap-assed nutty.
☺Note: Slap-ass Friday is becoming a popular tradition in middle schools where both sexes spank the other when opportunity presents.

The cheese slid off of that boy's cracker!
☺Rather than: I don't know whether to come home or go crazy.

The elevator don't go all the way to the top.
☺Fact: The high-speed elevators in Taipei 101, the world's tallest building, have a maximum speed of 37.6 mph.

The roof ain't nailed tight.
☺"Insanity doesn't run in my family; it gallops." Cary Grant

The wheels still turning, but the hamsters died.
☺"I hate to advocate drugs, alcohol, violence, or insanity to anyone, but they've always worked for me." Hunter S. Thompson

You don't have to hang from a tree to be a nut.
☺"Insanity is hereditary, you get it from your children." Sam Levenson

Deceased: Resting in peace in the marble orchard.

When University of Alabama football coach Paul (Bear) Bryant died in 1983, the funeral required three separate churches to handle the crush of mourners. Bryant's widow, family and dignitaries were seated in one church whose proceedings were piped through to two nearby churches. After the funeral service, the coffin was carried to a waiting hearse by eight pallbearers, all members of the 1982 Crimson Tide football team. A procession of 300 automobiles escorted by 19 motorcycle police and 7 police cars led the procession through campus, past the football stadium and then on to the Bryant family plot in Elmwood Cemetery in Birmingham 60 miles away. The burial was attended by more than 10,000 persons.

"That was a funeral in the finest tradition of the South," said Charles Wilson, professor of history and Southern studies at Ole Miss.

Don't forget to bring a nice casserole to the home of the bereaved, and don't forget these phrases.

Dead as iced catfish.
☺"Either this man is dead or my watch has stopped." Groucho Marx

Deader than a doornail.
☺Rather than: To come to a sticky end. Note: chiefly British.

Graveyard dead.
☺Rather than: To go to a Texas cakewalk.

Killed it dead.
☺Rather than: To kick the bucket

Resting in peace in the marble orchard.
☺Rather than: Sleeps with the fishes

<u>The gophers are nibbling at his toes.</u>
☺Rather than: He has assumed room temperature.

Dimwits: Dumber than a football bat.

Twitter is chock full of imbecility. There are hundreds of funny misspellings and word torture. For example, some folks have confused the word "cologne" with the word "colon". For example: "I love the smell of my boyfriend's colon (sic) on my pillow." Look those up later, here is a conversation an Australian friend of mine had in Manhattan.

- Girl: "I love your accent. Where are you from?" Aussy: "I'm Australian."

- Girl: "Australia, that's the ice continent isn't it?" Aussy: "No, you're thinking of Antarctica. Australia's north of that. South of Singapore. Kangaroos, boomerangs, shrimp on the barbi?"

- Girl: "No. It's an ice continent. Penguins, polar bears, and reindeer, right?" Aussie: "Shelia, Australia is temperate to tropical. Does Crocodile Dundee ring a bell?"

- Girl: "No, you're wrong. I read about it at school." Aussie: "Fine, I've lost my phone number, can I have yours? I need to call my igloo.

Southerners have funny ways of describing dimwits.

'Et up with the dumb-ass.
☺Rather than: Everyone has the right to do stupid things but you are abusing that privilege.

A few clowns short of a circus.
☺Rather than: One twist short of a slinky.

A few fire-logs short of a cord.
☺Rather than: Stupidity is not a crime so you are free to go.

A few fries short of a Happy Meal.
☺"An intelligent hell would be better than a stupid paradise."

Victor Hugo

A tree stump in a Louisiana swamp has a higher IQ.
☺"In politics, stupidity is not a handicap." Napoléon Bonaparte

About as sharp as a rat turd on both ends.
☺"There is more stupidity than hydrogen in the universe, and it has a longer shelf life." Frank Zappa

Couldn't get into college with a crowbar.
☺"TV and the Internet are good because they keep stupid people from spending too much time out in public." Douglas Coupland

Don't have sense enough to pound sand into a rat hole.
☺Rather than: I'm not fluent in IDIOT, so please speak s-l-o-w-l-y and clearly.

Doesn't have sense God gave an animal cracker.
☺"A foolish man tells a woman to stop talking, but a wise man tells her that her mouth is extremely beautiful when her lips are closed." English Proverb.

Dumb as a cat grooming itself in the middle of a dog festival.
☺Rather than: Anything too stupid to be said turns into a song.

Dumb enough for twins.
☺Rather than: Don't blame yourself. Let me do it!

Dumber than a box (bag, or barrel) of dirt. (Hair, hammers, doorknobs or rocks)
☺Rather than: Earnestness is stupidity sent to college.

Dumber than a football bat.
☺"There is nothing so stupid as the educated man if you get him off the thing he was educated in." Will Rogers

Dumber than a road lizard. (Brick, cabbage, fencepost, stump)

☺Rather than: Egotism is the anesthetic that dulls the pain of stupidity.

Empty as a winter rain barrel.
☺"The empty vessel makes the loudest sound." William Shakespeare

Empty wagons make the loudest noise.
☺Rather than: For two cents I'd give you a piece of my mind – and all of yours.

Engine is running, but nobody is driving.
☺Rather than: I couldn't repair your brakes, so I made your horn louder!

He ain't got the sense he was born with.
☺Rather than: I don't know what your problem is, but I bet it is hard to pronounce.

He ain't exactly setting the woods on fire.
☺Rather than: If I agreed with you, we'd both be wrong.

He ain't got the sense the good Lord gave a billy goat (or goose).
☺Rather than: In politics stupidity is not a handicap.

He ain't got the sense to lead a blind goose to shit.
☺Rather than: It's too bad that stupidity isn't painful.

He ain't the brightest Crayola in the box.
☺Rather than: Make it idiot proof and someone will create a better idiot.

He ain't the sharpest spoon in the drawer.
☺Rather than: He ain't the sharpest knife in the drawer.

He couldn't hit the broad side of a barn with a sail cat.
☺Note: A "sail cat" is road kill that has been flattened by several

vehicles.

Stupidity is a bus heading towards a cliff and everyone's arguing over where they're going to sit.
☺Also: He couldn't hit the ground if he fell twice!

He doesn't know "come here" from "sic 'em."
☺Rather than: Stupidity is the deliberate cultivation of ignorance.

He got stuck behind the door when they were handing out brains.
☺Note: Some people support bacteria, they are the only culture some people have.

He thought Grape Nuts was a venereal disease.
☺Rather than: The difference between genius and stupidity is that genius has limits.

He thought Peter Pan was a bed pan.
☺Rather than: The fact that no one understands you doesn't mean you're an artist.

He was casket sharp!
☺"The two most common elements in the universe are hydrogen and stupidity." Harlan Ellison

He's a few dogs shy of a hunt.
☺Rather than: He's so stupid… if you give him a penny for his thoughts, you'll get change back.

He's as lost as last year's Easter eggs.
☺"We are all born ignorant, but one must work hard to remain stupid." Benjamin Franklin

He's duller than a three-watt light bulb in a power outage.
☺"There is more stupidity than hydrogen in the universe and it has a much longer shelf life." Frank Zappa

He's got all the smarts God gave a duck's butt.
☺Rather than: Those who laugh last thinks slowest.

He's so dumb he couldn't find his ass with two hands and a flashlight.
☺Rather than: A wise man knows where courage ends and stupidity begins.

He's so dumb he couldn't piss his name in the snow.
☺"Only in Britain could it be thought a defect to be 'too clever by half.' The probability is that too many people are too stupid by three-quarters." John Major

He's so dumb he couldn't spell cat if you spotted him the "c" and the "t".
☺"I once dated a guy so dumb he could not count to 21 unless he was naked." Joan Rivers

He's so dumb he thinks Johnny Cash is a pay toilet.
☺"If there are no stupid questions, then what kind of questions do stupid people ask?"   Scott Adams

He's so dumb they had to burn down the school just to get him out of third grade.
☺"Stupidity, if left untreated, is self-correcting." Robert Heinlein

His brain rattles around like a BB in a boxcar.
☺"The difference between genius and stupidity is; genius has its limits." Alexandre Dumas

His cornbread ain't done.
☺"Your head is as empty as a hermit's address book." Rowan Atkinson

His porch light is out.
☺Rather than: What he lacks in intelligence, he makes up for in stupidity.

If brains were dynamite we wouldn't have enough to blow his nose.
☺"If stupidity got us into this mess, then why can't it get us out?"
Will Rogers

If brains were lard, he couldn't grease up a skillet.
☺Rather than: He is so dumb, blondes tell jokes about him.

If I put his brain in a gnat's butt, it would fly backwards.
☺"Nothing in the world is more dangerous than sincere ignorance
and conscientious stupidity." Martin Luther King Jr

If brains were leather, he wouldn't have enough to saddle a June-bug.
☺"Real stupidity beats artificial intelligence every time." Terry
Pratchett

If that boy had an idea it would die of loneliness.
☺Rather than: The fact that no one understands you doesn't mean
you're an artist.

Just about half-smart.
☺Rather than: He is so stupid… mind readers charge him half price.

Nice house, but no one's home.
☺Rather than: Your birth certificate is an apology letter from the
condom factory.

Not the sharpest spoon in the drawer.
☺"I'm very intelligent. I'm capable of doing everything put to me.
I've launched a perfume and want my own hotel chain. I'm living
proof blondes are not stupid." Paris Hilton

Plumb "et up" with the dumb ass.
☺"It's easy to identify people who can't count to ten; they're in
front of you in the supermarket express lane." June Henderson

Sharp as a bag of wet mice. (or wet liver)

☺Rather than: Is your ass jealous of the amount of shit that just came out of your mouth?

Sharp as a cue ball. (balloon, light-bulb, or marble)
☺Rather than: Wise people think all they say, fools say all they think.

So dumb he couldn't pour piss out of a boot with the instructions written on the heel.
☺Rather than: We have enough gun control. What we need is idiot control.

So dumb he took a duck to a chicken fight.
☺Rather than: Everyone has the right to be stupid, but he is abusing the privilege!

Strong like a bear and smart like a tractor.
☺Rather than: Build a machine any idiot can use, and only an idiot will want to use it.

That boy ain't the smartest peanut in the toilet.
☺Rather than: You are depriving some village of its idiot.

That boy's the nearest nothing.
☺Rather than: I refuse to have a battle of wits with an unarmed opponent.

Their brains in a thimble would roll like road apples in a bushel basket.
☺Rather than: Everyone has a photographic memory. Some just don't have film.

They are nine dimes short of a dollar.
☺Rather than: He may look like an idiot, and talk like an idiot, but don't let that fool you. He really is an idiot.

They think Cheerios are doughnut seeds!
☺Rather than: When it comes to thought, some people stop at

nothing.

Too many clowns, not enough circus.
☺"The trouble with the world is that the stupid are cocksure and the intelligent are full of doubt." Bertrand Russell

Won't get bowlegged by totting his brains.
☺Rather than: So far, I think nature is winning.

Your brain on the head of a pin would roll around like a BB on a six-lane highway.
☺Rather than: Some drink at the fountain of knowledge... Others just gargle.

Directions: Over yonder down the road a piece.

Southerner tend to navigate by landmark. You might hear this exchange if you ask for directions:

It's back there at the edge of nothing. Did you see the Sunoco Station back yonder? Turn there. You'll pass the old Sammon's place a piece down the road. Take a right at the first blinking light. You'll think you're lost, or leaving the country, just keep going. They'll be a fork in the road, take the right. A piece down that road you'll see a barn, then a church. After the graveyard take the next right. The house is the third on the left. It's so far out they have to pump in sunshine.

Here are the phrases to know for getting lost:

A piece down the road.
☺Meaning: About a mile or two.

I had to grease the wagon twice before hit the main road.
☺Meaning: About 4 hours.

Just a hop skip and a jump.
☺Meaning: About 30 minutes.

Just Over Yonder.
☺Meaning: There, where I would point if momma would let me.

Over yonder in the edge of nothing.
☺Meaning: You should have left last month.

Elderly: She has enough wrinkles to hold an eight day rain.

A friend of mine moved into a small Mississippi town from Chicago. He noticed that an elderly man down the street mowed his yard with a push mover. He would do a few rows, then mopping his brow, go onto the front porch to rest. When rested, he would go to push the mower a few rows, then break again. Mowing the yard would take most of the morning. My friend confided to another neighbor; that he was surprised no one helped. The response was, "Oh yes, Mr. Jim. For many years we've all but begged to mow it for him. He won't hear any of it. He wants to be self-sufficient.

If you see Mr. Jim on lawn days, here are the Southernisms you might use:

A little long in the tooth.
☺Rather then: Older than dirt in dog years.

Grandpa goes to bed with the chickens.
☺"Someday you will be old enough to start reading fairy tales again." C.S. Lewis

He ain't sawing logs, he's clearing brush.
☺Meaning: The old man is snoring loudly. "Laugh and the world laughs with you, snore and you sleep alone." Anthony Burgess

He was old back when Jesus was a boy.
☺Rather than: He knew dirt when it was still a rock.

He's about two years older than baseball.
☺"How old would you be if you didn't know how old you are?" Satchel Paige

He's as old as Methuselah.

☺"Old age is when you know all the answers, but nobody asks you the questions." Dr. Laurence J. Peter

I am as old as my tongue and a little older than my teeth.
☺"We don't stop playing because we grow old; we grow old because we stop playing." George Bernard Shaw

If he had one more wrinkle, he could screw his hat on.
☺"Remember that the most valuable antiques are dear old friends." H. Jackson Brown, Jr

Older than the mountains and got twice as much dust.
☺Fact: The Saint Francois Mountains of Missouri are the oldest in North America and were formed 1.4 Billion years ago.

Only thing alive at that house with all its teeth is the termites.
☺"She said she was approaching forty, and I couldn't help wondering from what direction." Bob Hope

She has enough wrinkles to hold an eight day rain.
☺I didn't see it (old age) coming — it hit me from the rear." Phyllis Diller

They've been around since dirt was new.
☺Fact: Most of the dirt you see today is from the past two million years, the oldest sedimentary rocks are about 3.9 billion years old.

Way back when I was knee-high to nothing.
☺"Years ago we discovered the exact point of middle age; it occurs when you are too young to take up golf and too old to rush up to the net." Franklin Adams

When grandpa was born, the Dead Sea was just sick.
☺Fact: An unusual feature of the Dead Sea is its discharge of asphalt. Asphalt coated figurines and skulls have been found locally.

Exclamations!: I swannie!

Many mothers and grandmothers will not use swear words, or even say the word "swear" - hence the term "swannie." You'll find the number of exclamations to be quite extraordinary. Some phrases are particular to states, counties, towns and even unique to families. Here are the exclamations you are most likely to hear.

Ain't that the berries!
☺Meaning: That is great!

Bless your pea picking little heart!
☺Rather than: Fragonard!

Cotton-picker!
☺Rather than: Fiddlesticks!

Damn Yankees!
☺Rather than: Jackhole.

Doesn't that just beat all you ever stepped in?
☺Rather than: What the whale?

Don't rush on my account!
☺Meaning: Hurry up dammit!"

Don't that take the rag off of the bush!
☺Rather than: Mothertrucker

Don't that just beat all you ever stepped in!
☺Rather than: Shut the front door!

For lands sake!
☺Rather than: Jerkstore!

Gad night a livin'!
☺Rather than: Sockmonkey!

Gather at the River!
☺Rather than: Holy Farking Schmit!

Going to Hell in a hand-basket!
☺Rather than: Sweet mother of God!

Good God almighty!
☺Rather than: Jeez of Nazareth!

Good heavenly days!
☺Rather than: Sweet Mother of God!

Great day in the morning!
☺Rather than: Mother of Macaulay Culkin!

Hellfire and damnation!
☺Rather than: Mother Scratch!

Hells' bells!
☺Rather than: Holy balls!

Hissy fit with a tail on it.
☺Rather than: Douche Nozzle!

I am losing my religion!
☺Rather than: Jiminy Christmas!

I declare!
☺Rather than: Holy Mackerel!

I do declare!
☺Rather than: Merciful Mother of our Blessed Lord!

I swannie!
☺Note: Many old folks would not say the word "swear."

I'll be dipped in shit and rolled in cracker crumbs!
☺Rather than: Butt cakes!

I'll dance at your wedding!
☺Note: Formerly meant "thank you", often used sarcastically today

I'll fly away Ole Glory!
☺Rather than: Chinese dentist!

If it ain't bedbugs it's piss ants!
☺Rather than: When it rains it pours.

In all my born days!
☺Rather than: Mother father!

Katie bar the door!
☺Rather than: Mother of Pearl!

Lord help me over the fence!
☺Rather than: Jesus H. Christ on a Popsicle stick!

Lord only knows – and he ain't telling!
☺Rather than: Jesus, Mary and Joseph!

Lordy Lordy who shot Shorty?
☺Rather than: Great God almighty.

My stars and garters!
☺Rather than: See You Next Tuesday.

Piss on that step ant!
☺Rather than: Note: Instead of "Step on that piss ant."

Quit hollering down the rain.

☺Rather than: Odds my bodkins!

Shit fire and save the matches!
☺Rather than: Shitake mushrooms!

Snap my garters!
☺Rather than: Well, box my nuts!

Stop that carrying on!
☺Rather than: Jiminy Cricket!

Swat my hind with a melon rind!
☺Rather than: Crapola!

Sweet fancy Moses on buttered toast!
☺Rather than: Crime in Italy!

That is just sor-reee. (Sorry)
☺Rather than: Holy Guacamole!

That makes my ass want a dip of snuff.
☺Rather than: Firgin Icehole!

That takes the rag off the bush.
☺Note: This refers to the practice of leaving one's clothes on a bush while skinny dipping. If else someone happened by, they might take your clothes, i.e. your 'rags' as a joke.

That sticks in my craw.
☺Rather than: Great Caesar's Ghost!

That's a fine how de' ya' do!
☺Rather than: Farfinpoopin!

Well color me stupid!
☺Rather than: Sugartit!

Well cut off my legs and call me shorty!
☺Rather than: Knock your socks off!

Well hush my mouth!
☺Rather than: Lo and behold!

Well I never!
☺Rather than: Jumpin' Jahosafat!

Well knock me down and steal my teeth!
☺Rather than: Oh Hell and Jesus Help Me Holy Ghost!

Well slap my head and call me silly!
☺Rather than: Heavens to Betsy!

Well thank you Billy Sunday!
☺Note: William "Billy" Sunday (1862 –1935) was a professional baseball player in the 1880s, and became the most celebrated and influential American evangelist early 20th century.

Well, go to war Miss Mitchell!
☺Note: The author of "Gone with the Wind", Margaret Mitchell.

What does that have to do with the price of tea in China?
☺Rather than: Well Helicopter!

What in tar-nation!
☺Rather than: Horse Hockey!

You scratch my back and I'll scratch yours.
☺Rather than: Tit for tat!

Excused: I need to see a man about a horse.

"Au revoir", "adios", "aloha" — there are plenty of ways to say goodbye, but it's not always easy to say "I gotta go." Hopefully, you don't find yourself in many situations where you need to announce your intentions. But just in case, here are the sayings to know.

I got to pee like a crippled goat.
☺Fact: Coffee is a diuretic - and goats discovered coffee beans.

I gotta go see a man about a horse.
☺Rather than: I gotta see a man about a goat, dog, or mule.

I gotta piss like a Russian race horse at the derby getting chased by a glue truck.
☺Fact: On Derby Day the infield will hold around 80,000 people, making it Kentucky's third-largest city, behind Lexington and Louisville.

I have to drop the Browns off at the Super Bowl.
☺Rather than: I've got to free a bog crocodile.

I hear a bull pissing on a flat rock.
☺Rather than: I'm off to shake hands with the unemployed.

I'm going to see the turtle take to water.
☺Rather than: Heave a Havana.

My eyeballs are floating.
☺Rather than: Free the trouser trout.

The only thing we got to fear is a public toilet seat.
☺Rather than: Lay down some spicy brown.

Glad: Happier than a dead pig in the sunshine.

The South is a rich gumbo of architecture, food, gardens, history, and music. But the people make it special. Southerners entertain easily. The table is always set for unexpected guests. Extra glasses wait on shady porches. People take time to visit. Families are treasured. Greetings like, "How's your momma n 'em?" are given considered response. Chances are you'll be happy when greeted; here are the way to express it.

Finer than frog's hair.
☺Rather than: On cloud nine.

Grinning like a mule eating briers over a barbwire fence.
☺Rather than: Happy as a clam.

Grinning like a possum eating grits out of a light socket.
☺Also: Happier than a baby in a barrel of tits.

Happier a preacher's son at a biker-babe rally!
☺Rather than: Happier than Dracula volunteering at a Blood Drive.

Happier than a dead pig in the sunshine.
☺Note: When pigs expire, their mouths curl back making them look like they are smiling.

Happier than a gopher in soft dirt.
☺Rather than: Happier than a butcher's dog.

Happier than a June-bug on a tomato plant.
☺Rather than: Happier than Gallagher at a farmer's market.

Happier than a pig in slop.
☺Rather than: Happier than a fat kid with a Twinkie.

Happier than a possum in the corn-crib.
☺Rather than: Happier than Dracula volunteering at a blood drive.

Happier than a puppy with two peckers.
☺Note: It's best to leave the extra penis be - it's a rare birth defect.

Happier than a tornado in a trailer park.
☺Rather than: Happier than a hurricane.

Happier than a water spaniel on a bare leg.
☺Rather than: Happier than a Corgi on stilts.

Happier than a woodpecker in a lumber yard.
☺Rather than: Happier than a camel on Wednesday.

Happy as a biker at the buffet.
☺Rather than: Happier than a zombie at a nursing home.

Happy as a tick on a fat dog.
☺Rather than: Happy as Warren Beatty's fingertips.

I haven't had this much fun since the pigs ate my brother.
☺Rather than: Happier than a slinky on an escalator.

I'm as giddy as a school girl on prom night.
☺Rather than: Happier than a witch in a broom factory.

I'm happier than a mule in a pickle patch.
☺Rather than: Happier than a midget at a mini-skirt convention.

I'm so tickled I can't get my leg down.
☺Rather than: Happier than the Pillsbury Dough-boy on his way to a baking convention.

If things get any better, I may have to hire someone to help me enjoy it.

☺Rather than: Happier than a billionaire in Costa Rica.

Goodbye: Don't let the door hit ya' where the Good Lord split ya'.

As a get-together winds down, some guests unwittingly overstay their welcome. I believe in erring on the side of under-staying – i.e. always leave them wanting more. How can you be sure when it's time to leave? A good host will provide clear clues: They take the wine bottle from your hand and recap it. They begin vacuuming the room. They excuse themselves to check on baby they don't have. They excuse themselves and return in pajamas. (Note: Exception made if a lady returns in a negligee.) As a last resort, your host sets off the fire sprinklers.

Here are the sayings to use in all but the negligee clue.

<u>Church is finally letting out.</u>
☺Rather than: I gotta jet.

<u>Church is out.</u>
☺Rather than: I gotta take off.

<u>Don't take any wooden nickels.</u>
☺Rather than: I gotta bounce.

<u>Don't let the door hit ya' where the good Lord split ya'.</u>
☺Rather than: I gotta split.

<u>Holler if you need me.</u>
☺Rather than: Don't cry because it's over. Smile because it happened.

<u>It's time to heat up the bricks.</u>
☺Rather than: Let the tidings of good fortune always clean up after itself.

It's time to put the chairs in the wagon.
☺Rather than: When your dreams turn to dust, it's time to vacuum.

It's time to swap spit and hit the road.
☺Rather than: It's all said and done, it's real, and it's been fun.

Keep your saddle oiled and your gun greased.
☺"History never really says goodbye. History says, 'See you later.'"
Eduardo Galeano

Let's blow this pop stand.
☺Rather than: Let's blow this joint.

Let's head for the wagon yard.
☺Rather than: I gotta make tracks.

Let's light a shuck.
☺Note: To get a mule to hurry back to the barn, farmers would light a cornhusk and tie it to the beast's tail.

Let's put some lipstick on this pig!
☺Fact: The phrase was introduced into contemporary usage in 1985 when a radio host San Francisco used the phrase reference to plans to refurbish Candlestick Park.

That about puts the rag on the bush.
☺Rather than: I gotta hit the road. Note: This refers to the practice of leaving ones' clothes on a bush while skinny dipping.

That's all she wrote.
☺Fact: The popular version of the origin of this expression is that it is the punch line of a mournful tale about an American GI serving overseas in WWII. The said sad serviceman is supposed to have received a letter from his sweetheart. He reads it to his colleagues: "Dear John". Well, go on, they say. "That's it; that's all she wrote".

Time to piss on the fire and call in the dogs.

☺Rather than: Smell you later.

Well, let me get on about my rat killin'.
☺Rather than: Peace out!

Y'all come back now, hear?
☺Note: From the Beverly Hillbillies: "Set a spell, take yer shoes off, y'all come back now, hear"

Gossip: I wouldn't pee in her ear if her brain was on fire.

My neighborhood's real-estate agent and self-appointed moralist was known as for her unsolicited opinions of other's private lives. When asked why this was her business, she would inevitably refer to my neighborhood as her "farm." The community was offended by this busybody, but feared being the focus of her attention, so we all tried to ignore her.

One day the real-estate agent set her spyglass on me. She reported to my neighbors that my Hummer parked in front of a strip club. Her comments got back to my wife.

For the rest of the week, I parked my car in front of her house overnight. I heard she had no problem selling her house.

Gossip is unavoidable I'm afraid. We all do it, here's how to comment Southern style.

A little powder, a little paint, makes a girl look what she ain't!
☺Meaning: Watch out for high maintenance later on.

A person to go to the well with.
☺"The trite saying that honesty is the best policy has met with the just criticism that honesty is not policy. The real honest man is honest from conviction of what is right, not from policy."   Robert E. Lee

"Big hat, no cattle.
☺Meaning: Full of big talk, and lacking action or substance, but pretentious all the same.

Call him an idiot and you'll insult all the idiots in the world.
☺Note: 2% of the world's population has an IQ under 70. I think I've worked for all of them.

Couldn't find his own ass with both hands stuck in his back pockets.
☺"Never ascribe to malice that which can adequately be explained by incompetence." Napoleon Bonaparte

Couldn't punch his way out of a wet paper bag.
☺"If at first you don't succeed, you may be at your level of incompetence already." Dr. Laurence J. Peter

Drove her ducks to a poor puddle.
☺"Nobody ever did, or ever will, escape the consequences of his choices." Alfred A. Montapert

Everything she's got is out on the showroom floor.
☺Meaning: She is wearing a revealing outfit.

Fish stinks from the head down.
☺Meaning: Organizations reflect their leaders. "This proverb is of ancient origin, Greek and Chinese cultures lay claim to it."

He got weaned from sucking eggs.
☺Meaning: To learn the hard way.

He'll stand the hedge and take up the gap.
☺The term is from the Civil War and referees to "set piece: method of fighting – i.e. not using cover.

He's so low down he could crawl under a snake's belly.
☺"He was distinguished for ignorance; for he had only one idea and that was wrong." Benjamin Disraeli

His family tree ain't got branches.
☺Rather than: Ever since I saw you in your family tree I've wanted to cut it down.

He's so honest you could shoot craps with him over the phone.
☺"I hope I shall possess firmness and virtue enough to maintain what I consider the most enviable of all titles, the character of an

honest man." George Washington

He was so deep in jail he'll have to be fed beans with a sling-shot!
☺Note: It might be a good thing to leave him back there. Other foods that have "flatulence factors" are cabbage, eggs and beer.

He'd complain if you hung him with a new rope.
☺Fact: Execution by hanging is generally performed with a rope that has been prepared by boiling and drying under tension. New rope tends to coil, which causes it to act like a spring as it supports the weight of the body during hanging. This is at best undignified, and at worst likely to interfere with the effectiveness of the procedure.

He'd gripe with a ham under each arm.
☺Note: The only similarity between southern country ham and the stuff in the deli case is that they both require pig sacrifice. To southerners and pork devotees, country ham is exquisite dry-cured rosy-hued perfection itself.

He'd put a rattlesnake in your pocket and ask you for a light.
☺"Those are my principles If you don't like them I have others."
Groucho Marx

He's the cream of the crap, and the crap of the cream.
☺Meaning: He is a real shit.

He's a hard dog to keep under the porch.
☺Note: Make famous by Ms. Clinton in the .Lewinsky affair."

He's gone back on his raisin'.
☺Meaning: That he has turned his back on his heritage or good upbringing.

Her hair looks like it caught on fire and somebody put it out with a brick.
☺"My photographs don't do me justice - they just look like me."
Phyllis Diller

Her jeans are so tight, you can see Washington grinning on the quarter in her pocket.
☺"Blue jeans are the most beautiful things since the gondola."
Diana Vreeland

His pants were so tight that if he farted, he'd blow his boots off.
☺Note: A man is most likely to be flatulent first thing in the morning, AKA "morning thunder".

I hate her stomach for carrying her guts.
☺"She's afraid that if she leaves, she'll become the life of the party."
Grouch Marx

I wouldn't pee in her ear if her brain was on fire.
☺Fact: Two to three drops of urine will cure an ear ache.

If she had one more wrinkle, she could screw her hat on.
☺Note: An old superstition says never lay your hat on a bed - it means someone will die.

It must be jelly because jam don't shake like that.
☺"Here's to our wives and girlfriends may they never meet!"
Groucho Marx

I can tell you a thing or two 'bout a thing or two.
☺Note: When wearing a bikini, women reveal 90% of their body....men are so polite they only look at the covered parts.

I don't think he has enough chlorine in his gene pool.
☺Rather than: He was the poster child for birth control.

I wouldn't walk across the street to piss on him if he was on fire.
☺Note: One can put out a fire by urinating, but it depends on the size of the fire, and size of the hose.

Jesus loves him, but that's about it.

☺Rather than: Time wounds all heels.

Just between you, me, and the fence post.
☺"Anyone who says he can see through women is missing a lot."
Groucho Marx

Just wear beige and keep quiet.
☺Note: If all mother-in-laws followed this advice there would be no
need for mother-in-law jokes.

Lives like a fighting cock.
☺Meaning: He lives like there is no tomorrow.

Looks like two Buicks fighting for a parking place.
☺Note: Like middle aged woman in tight yoga pants at the yogurt
bar.

Momma's baby - Daddy's maybe.
☺Note: There are no illegitimate children - only illegitimate parents.

No weevils in his wheat.
☺Meaning: A very honest person. "Honor lies in honest toil."
Grover Cleveland

Rabbit running through the briar patch and don't know which one
stuck it.
☺Meaning: She sleeps around and father unknown.

She always looks like she stepped out of a band box.
☺Note: The "Band Box" was a euphemistic slang expression for a
notorious brothel frequented by Union soldiers on the grounds of the
current IRS building in Washington, D.C.

She could depress the devil.
☺"I've had a perfectly wonderful evening but this wasn't it."
Grouch Marx

She could make a preacher cuss.
☺"Meaning: Someone who might also argue with a stop sign.

She looks like death sitting on tombstones hatching haints.
☺Note: "Haints" are a Southern expression for ghosts.

She wouldn't go to a funeral unless it was theirs.
☺Rather than: Everyone has an ego, mine is just bigger...and better.

She's a caution.
☺"A woman scorned is a woman who quickly learns her way around a courtroom." Colette Mann

She's an iron hand in a velvet glove.
☺"Put your iron hand in a velvet glove." Napoléon Bonaparte

She's got more nerve than Carter's got Liver Pills.
☺Note: Carter's Little Liver Pills were formulated as a patent medicine by Samuel J. Carter of Erie, Pennsylvania in 1868. The active ingredient is bisacodyl. The FDA forced "Liver" to be dropped in the name in 1959.

She's must have eleven-teenth kids.
☺"The main reason Santa is so jolly is because he knows where all the bad girls live." George Carlin

She's so stuck up, she'd drown in a rainstorm.
☺"I'm not conceited. Conceit is a fault and I have no faults." David Lee Roth

She's so sweet; sugar wouldn't melt in her mouth.
☺"She looked as though butter wouldn't melt in her mouth – or anywhere else." Elsa Lanchester

She's wilder than a fifth ace.
☺"Women should be obscene and not heard." Groucho Marx

She's as welcome as a skunk at a lawn party.
☺"If a woman likes another woman, she's cordial; if she doesn't like her, she's very cordial." Irvin Cobb

She's as wild as a peach orchard boar.
☺"Remember men, you are fighting for this lady's honor; which is probably more than she ever did." Groucho Marx

She's been storked.
☺Meaning: Storked = Pregnant. "To me life is tough enough without having someone kick you from the inside." Rita Rudner

She's dancing in the hog trough.
☺"When she was pregnant, she would get these cravings in the middle of the night… for other men." Brian Kiley

She's itching for something she won't scratch for.
☺"It takes a woman twenty years to make a man of her son, and another woman twenty minutes to make a fool of him." Helen Rowland

She's sitting below the salt.
☺"Politics doesn't make strange bedfellows, marriage does." Groucho Marx

Sorry as a two dollar watch.
☺Note: EBay has around 100K watches for $2.99 or less.

Straight as a string.
☺"Tricks and treachery are the practice of fools, that don't have brains enough to be honest." Benjamin Franklin

Still wet behind your ears.
☺Note: "Wet behind the ears," meaning inexperienced or naive. Behind the ears is the last part of a foal or calf to dry out after birth.

That girl is like a doorknob - everyone gets a turn.

☺Good girls are bad girls that never get caught.

That woman learned how to whisper in a saw mill.
☺"Old maids sweeten their tea with scandal." Josh Billings

The higher the hair, the closer to God.
☺"People always ask me how long it takes to do my hair. I don't know, I'm never there." Dolly Parton

There might be all kinds, but I'm not sure it takes all kinds.
☺Meaning: I am not going to tolerate that person

They are as welcome as an outhouse breeze.
☺Rather than: The welcome mat said, "Oh no, not you again."

They ate supper before they said grace.
☺Rather than: Sex is not the answer. Sex is the question. "Yes" is the answer.

They never could set horses.
☺Meaning: They could never get along.

Wasn't nothin' between him and the Lord but a smile.
☺"If I held you any tighter, I'd be on the other side of you." Groucho Marx

Wild as a mink.
☺Note: The American mink is a promiscuous animal, which does not form pair bonds. The mating season lasts for three weeks. Mating process is violent, with the male typically biting the female on the nape of the neck and pinning her with his forefeet and can last up to 4 hours.

You can bet the farm on it.
☺"No such thing as a man willing to be honest - that would be like a blind man willing to see." F. Scott Fitzgerald

<u>You can hang your hat on it.</u>
☺"Dare to be honest and fear no labor."   Robert Burns

<u>You can take that to the bank.</u>
☺"<u>Honest conviction is my courage; the Constitution is my guide.</u>"
<u>Andrew Johnson</u>

<u>You can't hold water.</u>
Meaning: You can't keep a secret.

Greetings and Responses: Bless your pea-picking heart.

In linguistics, the Yankee phrase "How are you doing?" or more often "Howyadoin!", is called a phatic expression. Its' function is to perform a social task, as opposed to seeking information. You might be familiar with the Mandarin greeting "nǐ chīfàn le ma" which translates to "Have you eaten?" The proper response to a phatic expression is to repeat it to the speaker. Here are a few others: Georgia:"Let you win", Iceland:"Happy", Mauritania:"On you no evil", Mauritius:"Speak!" Micronesia: "It was good", Swaziland:" I see you!"

In the North, "Howyadoin!" has also lost its' literal meaning, but in the South, you are expected to reply. Here are the Greetings and responses to use.

Aren't you precious?
☺Rather than: So what brings you here?

Been chewed up and spit out.
☺"It's a little like wrestling a gorilla; you don't quit when you're tired, you quit when the gorilla is tired."   Robert Strauss

Better than snuff and ain't half as dusty.
☺Note: This refers to dry nasal snuff popular in the 17-19th centuries.

Bright-eyed and bushy-tailed.
☺Rather than: What it do, home skillet?

Did Ford stop making trucks?
☺Meaning: Why so sad. On April 25, 1925 the Ford Motor Company introduced their first factory produced pickup truck, officially called the Ford Model T Runabout with Pickup Body.

Every thing's chicken but the bill.
☺Don't even think about not saying "hi".

Fair to Middlin'.
☺Meaning: Just above average. It is a farming term rooted in 18th century England.

Fine as a frog's hair split up the middle and tied at both ends. (Or split three ways)
☺What's shakin' bacon?

Fine as a frog's hair split up the middle and tied at both ends.
☺Note: Amphibian hard is very fine indeed. This is a very happy person.

Fit as a Fiddle.
☺"The only way to keep your health is to eat what you don't want, drink what you don't like, and do what you'd rather not."   Mark Twain

Gimme a yankee dime!
☺Meaning: Give me a kiss.

Gone to the Yankees.
☺Meaning: Worn out.

Gooder'n snuff (or grits).
☺Rather than: Sup frylock?

Happier than a pig in shit.
☺"Happiness is nothing more than good health and a bad memory." Albert Schweitzer

Happier than two dead pigs in the sunshine.
☺Note: The "smile" is caused by the fleshy mouth parts of a pig curling back in rigor mortis.

Haven't seen you in a minute.
☺Rather than: What's shakin' bacon?

He looks like 10 miles of bad road.
☺"I'm not good and tired, just tired." Mae West

He's got a hitch in his get-a-long.
☺"My doctor recently told me that jogging could add years to my life. I think he was right. I feel ten years older already." Milton Berle

How's your Momma n' Em?
☺Note: The Southern way to ask, "How is your entire family?"

I feel like a can of mashed assholes.
☺"You never get tired unless you stop and take time for it." Bob Hope

I feel like I been eaten by a wolf and shit over a cliff.
☺Also: You look like you were pulled through a knothole backwards.

I feel like I got eaten by a bear and shit off a cliff.
☺"After five days in hospital, I took a turn for the nurse." Spike Milligan

I feel like I was rode hard and put away wet.
☺"You should consult my doctor, you won't live to regret it." Larry Schwimmer

I was born tired and I've since suffered a relapse.
☺Fact: A typical energy drink contains about the same amount of caffeine as a cup of coffee.

I'm doing as little as possible and the easy ones twice.
☺Rather than: Yo baby pickle!

I'm so sick I'd have to get better to die.
☺"First the doctor told me the good news: I was going to have a disease named after me." Steve Martin

If I knew you was coming, I'd have baked a cake!☺Note: The title of a 1950 hit record by Eileen Barton, the phrase quickly caught on, and was common with people who grew up in the 50's and 60's.

If I was any happier I'd be twins.
☺Meaning: You're happy enough for two people.

I'm all wool and a yard wide.
☺Note: Meaning "doing great". Cloth made of 100% wool and in yard widths was best for hand tailors to work on. This was considered the criteria for excellence.

I'm bowed up like a Halloween cat.
☺"It's no longer a question of staying healthy. It's a question of finding a sickness you like." Jackie Mason

I'm hanging in there like loose teeth.
☺Meaning: Doing good

I'm keeping it between the ditches.
☺Rather than: Later gater.

Lick that calf again?
☺Meaning: Say that again?

Like 5 gallons of shit in a 2 gallon bucket.
☺"Quit worrying about your health. It'll go away." Robert Orben

Like a dog with two tails.
☺Note: meaning: "happy", this phrase is probably English in origin.

Look what the cat drug up!

☺Note: By leaving a dead animal on the back porch, cats act out their natural role as teacher. You represent her surrogate litter. The cat knows you would never have been able to catch that mouse on your own.

Petered out.
☺"A conclusion is simply the place where you got tired of thinking." Dan Chaon

Plumb tuckered out.
☺"A bicycle can't stand on its own because it is two-tired." Barry Popik

Puddin' tain...ask me again and I'll tell you the same!
☺Note: Answer to the question, "What's your name?"

Right as rain.
☺Note: Right as rain emerged in the 19th century. It became popular because of its pleasing alliteration, and because rain is good as it enables growth.

Rode hard and put up wet.
☺"I told him I wasn't tired; he told me, 'No, but the outfielders sure are." MLB pitcher, Jim Kern

Set a spell.
☺Note: First written in 1876, Louisa May Alcott, "The Romance of a Summer Day"

Sick as a dog passing peach pits.
☺Fact: Dogs will eat just about anything: batteries, Vaseline, and yes, peaches whole.

Still kickin' but not high, still floppin' but can't fly.
☺Meaning: I'm doing just okay - not quite average."

We get along like a house on fire!

☺Note: This phrase has been around since the mid-1700s, and means - as fast as a house would burn; very rapidly or vigorously.

Went to the outhouse and the hogs ate him.
☺Meaning: I don't know where that person is.

Who licked the red off your candy?
☺Fact: Red food coloring is the most commonly used dye in the U.S, and is synthetically derived from petroleum.

Who pissed in your Wheaties?
☺Fact: The first athlete to appear on a Wheaties box was Lou Gehrig in 1934 - he appeared on the back, not on the front.

Worn to a frazzle.
☺Note: Never argue with a women when she's tired – or rested.

You little cotton-picker!
☺Fact: The cotton picking world record is 910 pounds picked in nine hours set in 1925 by George

You're a sight for sore eyes!
☺Meaning: Glad to see you. Appropriate to say to the tow-truck driver as well.

Homely: His mother had to borrow another baby for church.

If you've been transferred to Charleston SC, you won't be needing these sayings, but if you travel to Philadelphia you just might.

In 2013 and for the third year in a row, Philadelphia ranked as ugliest US city by Travel and Leisure. Travel and Leisure also ranked Philly dead last in the "attractive people" category, extremely unfriendly (26th out of 30), and not the least bit athletic (28th out of 30).

You might be thinking I could make a lot of jokes about Philly's plight. You'd be correct - but I'm confident my wife already thinks I'm funny and I have a deadline to meet. Just in case you're in Philly on business, here are the sayings you'll want handy.

<u>About as sexy as socks on a billy goat.</u>
☺Fact: Of the many reasons to own a goat: milk, lawn moving, companionship, etc... home security is often mentioned. Yes, that would be a "watch goat."

<u>As ugly as a stack of black cats with their tails cut off.</u>
☺Ugly as a moose chewin' ice.

<u>Beauty is only skin deep, but ugly goes right to the bone.</u>
☺"She has a face like a saint – a St. Bernard!"   Rodney Dangerfield

<u>Born short and slapped flat.</u>
☺Rather than: When they walk by a toilet it flushes itself.

<u>Has to sneak up on a fountain to get a drink.</u>
☺Rather than: She has got 10 foot pole marks all over her.

<u>Has to sneak up on a water fountain to get a drink.</u>
☺"Never pick a fight with an ugly person, they've got nothing to

lose."   Robin Williams

He could scare a rat off a cheesecake.
☺Rather than: When he goes swimming the tide goes out.

He didn't get hit with the ugly stick; he got whooped with the whole forest!
☺Note: One of the all-time great comebacks. "I may be drunk madam, but in the morning I will be sober and you will still be ugly."   Winston Churchill

He fell out of the ugly tree and hit every branch on the way down.
☺Rather than: Everybody has the right to be ugly, but you abused the privilege.

He looks like he has been suckin' a sow!
☺"When I was born I was so ugly the doctor slapped my mother." Rodney Dangerfield

He looks like something the dog has been keeping under the porch.
☺"Beauty may be skin deep, but ugly goes clear to the bone."   Redd Foxx

He looks like something the dog's been keeping under the porch.
☺"When I answer the door the kids hand me candy."   Rodney Dangerfield

He looks like three pounds of ugly in a two-pound sack.
☺Rather than: His parents named him Shit Happens.

He must have been inside the outhouse when lightning struck.
☺Rather than: When he throws a boomerang it won't come back.

He stuck his finger in a light socket while his mama was beating him with an ugly stick.
☺"Joe Frazier is so ugly that when he cries, the tears turn around and go down the back of his head."   Muhammad Ali

He was so buck toothed he could eat an apple through a keyhole.
☺"I said to a bartender, Make me a zombie. He said "God beat me to it." Rodney Dangerfield

He's so ugly his cooties have to close their eyes.
☺Rather than: Did your parents have any children that lived?

He's so cross-eyed he can stand on the front porch and count chickens in the backyard.
☺"So I'm ugly. So what? I never saw anyone hit with his face." Yogi Berra

Her behind is big as the Buckeye fence.
☺"Have you ever seen people so ugly that you have to get someone else to verify it?" Jeff Foxworthy

Her hair was fried, dyed and laid to the side.
☺Rather than: She has a nice butter face. Everything looks nice, but her face.

His eyes were so crossed; he could keep one eye on the snake and look for a stick with the other eye.
☺"Lot of ugly funny dudes end up with some pretty gorgeous women. Women are much deeper than us in choosing a mate - they see in the long term." Patton Oswalt

His momma had to tie a pork chop around her neck to get the dogs to play with them.
☺Rather than: When he walked in to Taco Bell, everyone ran for the border.

His mother borrowed another baby for baptism.
☺Rather than: His parents asked him to run away from home?

I wonder what she would charge to haunt a house?
☺Rather than: When she walks into a haunted house, she came out

with a paycheck.

If you fell into a pond, you could skim off ugly for a week.
☺"She was known as a two bagger; that's when a girl is so ugly that you put a bag over your head in case the bag over her bag breaks."
Rodney Dangerfield

It takes a whole lotta liquor to like her.
☺Rather than: Any similarity between you and a human is purely coincidental.

Last time I saw a mouth like that it had a bit in it.
☺Rather than: If you are going to be two faced, at least make one of them pretty.

Looks like he sorts bobcats for a living.
☺Rather than: The last time I saw a face like yours I fed it a banana.

Looks like he was pulled through a knothole backwards.
☺Rather than: You must have been born on a highway because that's where most accidents happen.

Looks like ten miles of bad road.
☺Rather than: The only way you'll ever get laid is if you crawl up a chicken's ass and wait.

Mama takes him everywhere she goes so she doesn't have to kiss him goodbye.
☺"My doctor told me that I'm old, fat, and ugly, but none of those things is going to kill me immediately." Roger Ailes

Plain as a river slug.
☺Fact: A slug can stretch out to 20 times its normal length.

She could scare the bulldog off a meat truck.
☺Rather than: The proctologist stuck his finger in her mouth.

She had a face so ugly she wore out two bodies.
☺Rather than: When she gets up, the sun goes down.

She looks like her face caught fire and somebody put it out with an ice pick.
☺Rather than: Oh my God, look at you. Was anyone else hurt in the accident?

She looks like she got hit in the face with a sackful of bent nickels.
☺Rather than: Her father carries around the picture of the kid who came with his wallet.

She looks like she got hit in the face with rock salt.
☺Rather than: You are proof that God has a sense of humor.

She looks like she plays goalie for a dart team.
☺Rather than: Your mother had morning sickness—after you were born.

She looks like she ran a forty-yard dash in a thirty-yard gym.
☺Rather than: What are you going to do for a face when the baboon wants his butt back?

She was so ugly she looked like her face caught fire and someone beat it out with a track shoe.
☺"I do not know if she was virtuous, but she was ugly, and with a woman that is half the battle." Heinrich Heine

She's ugly enough to stop an eight-day clock.
☺Rather than: She can sink her face in dough and make monster cookies.

So short when farts he blows dirt into his pockets.
☺Rather than: He can sit on a curb and swing his legs.

So ugly he'd scare a buzzard off a gut pile.
☺Rather than: Did your parents ever ask you to run away from home?

So ugly she'd make a freight train take a dirt road.
☺Rather than: She's so ugly she makes onions cry.

So ugly they had to trick or treat over the telephone.
☺Rather than: I could make a monkey out of you, but why should I take all the credit?

So ugly when she was a baby her mom fed her with a slingshot.
☺Fact: The slingshot was invented in Russia, and was originally made from antlers

Somebody broke the ugly stick over his head.
☺Rather than: He is dark and handsome. When it's dark, he's handsome.

Stump-hole ugly.
☺Rather than: Someone left a cage open.

That baby is so ugly, when he was born the doctor slapped his Mama.
☺"A hooker once told you she had a headache." Rodney Dangerfield

That boy is so ugly he couldn't get laid in a whore house with a fist full of hundreds.
☺"A woman is an occasional pleasure but a cigar is always a smoke." Groucho Marx

That face might not stop a clock, but it'd sure raise Hell with watches.
☺Note: The saying is from the 1870s

Their momma had to be drunk to breastfeed them!
☺Fact: Alcohol passes freely into mother's milk and has been found to peak about 30 to 60 minutes after consumption, 60 to 90 minutes when taken with food.

They couldn't hem up a pig in a corner.

☺Note: Pigs are intelligent, gregarious and hedonistic. They are also curious. Being both intelligent and curious can prove problematic for keeping pigs as pets.

They have a face for radio.
☺Rather than: And a voice for Twitter

Uglier than a lard bucket full of armpits.
☺Rather than: She entered an ugly contest the judges said, "No professionals."

Ugly as a mud fence daubed with tadpoles.
☺Rather than: Don't let an extra chromosome get your down.

Ugly as homemade lye soap.
☺Note: Commercial lye is Sodium Hydroxide, which is often used in drain openers. Homemade lye is Potassium Hydroxide, which is mild and can be made at home from wood ashes.

Ugly enough to stop a bucket of snot in mid-air.
☺Note: During the age of sail, sailor on warships commented that the vessel itself seemed to be "surprised" when ambushed by another ship.

How Much? By the skin of my teeth.

The magic of Southern speech is in the similes and metaphors and other allusions. These techniques are the yellow highlighter of conversation. Could one communicate without the color commentary? Sure, one could live on bread and water too, but in the South there is no need. Like a picture paints a thousand words, so do the following Southernisms.

As country as Corn Flakes.
☺Fact: The accidental invention of corn flakes goes back to 1894 when a group of Seventh-day Adventists developed a new food to adhere to their vegetarian diet.

As slick as cat shit on linoleum.
☺Fact: Linoleum was invented by Englishman Frederick Walton. In 1855, Walton happened to notice the rubbery, flexible skin of solidified linseed oil (linoxyn) that had formed on a can of oil-based paint, and thought that it might form a substitute for India rubber.

As welcome as an outhouse breeze.
☺Rather than: Knee deep and sinking fast.

Barefooted as a yard dog.
☺Rather than: Since ditching shoes, I no longer suffer from foot odor.

Better than a sharp stick in the eye.
☺Fact: Your eye is about the size of a gum ball, and the lens the size of an M&M.

Bleeding like a stuck pig.
☺Fact: To avoid tainting the meat, the throat of a pig to be slaughtered is cut by severing the jugular vein

Bowed up like a Banty rooster.
☺Note: Bantams are about 1/4 the size of a "regular" chicken and are bred for cockfighting.

Brave as a bigamist.
☺Fact: In the Maldives, bigamy is permitted for anyone, most other Middle Eastern countries require you be a Muslim.

Brave as the first man to eat an oyster.
☺Fact: Scientists exploring a cave in South Africa report evidence of shellfish dinners enjoyed by humans who lived 164,000 years ago.

Brave enough to eat in the boomtown saloon.
☺Note: The "free lunch" was offered to attract customers who had to purchase at least one drink. The term first appeared in the 1870s.

By the skin of my teeth.
☺Note: The phrase first appears in English in the Geneva Bible, 1560, in Job 19:20, which provides a literal translation of the original Hebrew:" I haue escaped with the skinne of my tethe."(sic)

Clean as a hound's tooth.
☺Note: Contrary to myth, a dogs' mouth is equally dirty as humans.

Common as goat nuts.
☺Fact: The testicles of calves, lambs, roosters, turkeys, and other animals are eaten in many parts of the world, under a wide variety of euphemistic culinary names.

Cooler than the other side of the pillow.
☺Fact: Charlotte Thomas' "Bespoke" linens weave 22k gold thread into thousand-count Egyptian cotton. A set goes for around $2,400.

Country as a baked bean sandwich!
☺Note: Add a big slice of onion, and stay home for the evening.

Dark as a sack of black cats.

☺Note: Most of Europe considers the black cat a symbol of bad luck, except for the Scots. Go figure

Dark as the inside of a cow.
☺"My wife was afraid of the dark… then she saw me naked and now she's afraid of the light." Rodney Dangerfield

Deaf in one ear and can't hear out of the other.
☺"A good marriage would be between a blind wife and a deaf husband." Michel de Montaigne

Even a blind man on a galloping horse could see it.
☺Meaning: So obvious it could not be missed.

Flashy as a rat with a gold tooth.
☺Meaning: Ostentatious, showy and a bit too flashily dressed.

Flatter than a fritter.
☺Note: A "fritter" is a pancake made with corn meal.

Forty going north.
☺Meaning: Into middle age. Listen to Jimmy Buffett's "Pirate Looks at Forty."

Going at it like killing snakes.
☺Meaning: To do something with a great deal of energy.

Good enough for state work.
☺Meaning: Do the job just good enough.

Green as a gourd.
☺Fact: One of the earliest domesticated the bottle gourd has been discovered in archaeological sites dating from as early as 13,000 BC.

Grinning like a possum eating a sweet potato.
☺Note: Possums eat just about anything they can catch, or that has expired. A sweet potato would be a sweet treat.

Harder than a wedding pecker.
☺Note: No need to explain this one.

He ain't sawing logs, he's clearing brush.
☺Meaning: Snoring loudly.

He looked like a pig on ice.
☺Meaning: Funny and ungraceful.

He talks like he's got a mouthful of mush.
☺"I know that you believe you understand what you think I said, but I'm not sure you realize that what you heard is not what I meant."
Robert McCloskey

He thinks he's the best thing since sliced bread.
☺Fact: Bread has been used since the 17th century to clean the frescoes on the ceiling of the Sistine Chapel, Wonder Bread proved to be an especially effective sponge in the restoration of Michelangelo's masterpiece.

He thinks the sun come up just to hear him crow.
☺Note: Why roosters seem to love to crow anytime, including mornings, isn't fully understood.

He was so fat it was easier to go over top of him than around him.
☺Fact: The average American male weighs 191 lbs.

He was the turd in the punchbowl.
☺Meaning: Something which ruins or spoils everything else; a nuisance or problem; an unpleasant or disagreeable detail.

He's so deaf, he can't hear himself fart.
☺Note: Say what you want about deaf people.

He's so scared you couldn't drive a wet watermelon seed up his butt with a sledge hammer.

☺Rather than: So scared, the heads in the fridge begin to chant.

He's so thin-skinned, it's just barely enough to keep him from bleeding to death.
☺Note: Why is it so hard for women to find men that are sensitive, caring, and good-looking? Because those men already have boyfriends.

He's scratched up worse than a blind berry picker.
☺Fact: Blackberry tea was a cure for dysentery during the Civil War; during outbreaks, temporary truces were declared to allow soldiers to go "blackberrying".

He's shaking like an old dog shittin' logging chains. (Hammer handles or peach seeds)
☺Rather than: Shaking like a yellow Jell-O.

He's so country he thinks a seven-course meal is a possum and a six-pack.
☺Note: An old recipe goes: roast possum with a brick. When the possum is done, throw it away and eat the brick.

Heavier than a dead preacher.
☺Rather than: Heavy as a boarding-house dumpling.

High as giraffe nuts.
☺Note: Male giraffe's perform a procedure known as the "fleshmen sequence" to see if the female is in estrus. Males nudge the female's rump to induce urination, then take a mouthful of urine. If it tastes right he begins to court her.

I bought it for a song and you can sing it yourself.
☺Meaning: I bought it cheaply and will prove it.

I don't know her from Adam's house-cat.
☺Note: This expression has so long been a familiar idiom that people have felt the need to make it more emphatic. Speakers in

various parts of the US have at times commented they don't know somebody from Adam's house-cat, Adam's brother, Adam's foot, and Adam's pet monkey.

I was never like this until I was born.
☺"The two most important days in your life are the day you are born and the day you find out why."   Mark Twain

I was stuck hub deep to a Ferris wheel.
☺Fact: The original Ferris Wheel was designed and constructed by George Washington Gale Ferris, Jr. as a landmark for the 1893 World's Columbian Exposition in Chicago.

I'm sweating like a whore in church.
☺Rather than: Sweating like a politician on a polygraph.

I'm up shit creek without a paddle.
☺Fact: The Union Secretary of War said in a transcript, "Our men have put old Abraham Lincoln up shit creek."

I'm just hanging out like a hair in a biscuit.
☺Meaning: A little out of place.

I'm out like a fat kid in dodge-ball.
☺Note: Dodge ball is played the collegiate level in Europe.

I'm prouder of that than a pup with his first flea.
☺Fact: Fleas feed once every day or two, and generally remain on their host during the interim.

If that don't tickle your fancy, I'll kiss your ass until your hat flies off.
☺Note: One of the earliest known references comes from Abraham Tucker's 1774 In the Light of Nature Pursued, the author tells of animals "whose play had a quality of striking the joyous perception, or, as we vulgarly, say, tickling the fancy."

It was hanging open like a pea-coat sleeve.

☺Note: A "pea-coat" is tailored from "pilot cloth" – a stout, twilled blue cloth with the nap on one side. Then P-cloth, P-jacket – later a pea coat.

It's a right far piece from here.
☺Meaning: Closer than East Jesus, yet farther than yonder.

It's plain as a pig on a sofa.
☺Note: The phrase is attributed to Flannery O'Connor

It's quieter than a mouse pissing on cotton.
☺Note: A great gray owl can hear a mouse pissing on cotton 60 feet away.

It's more than I can say grace over.
☺Note: The word 'grace' literally means 'favor' In Hebrew.

Just a hop skip and a jump.
☺"Traveling is like flirting with life. It's like saying, 'I would stay and love you, but I have to go; this is my station.'" Lisa St. Aubin de Terán

Knee high to a grasshopper.
☺ Fact: Grasshopper species which change color and behavior at high population densities are called locusts.

Like a garlic milkshake.
☺Meaning: Smooth and strong.

Like a polecat at a camp meeting.
☺Note: In the US, the term "polecat" is sometimes applied to the black-footed ferret, and loosely to skunks.

Like a popcorn fart in Hell.
☺Meaning: I'm being ignored. A popcorn fart is dry and non-odiferous.

Like a rooster in an empty hen-house.
☺"Expectation is the mother of all frustration."   Antonio Banderas

Like a rubber nosed woodpecker in a petrified forest.
☺Meaning: Frustrated. Note: The ivory-billed woodpecker is one of the largest woodpeckers in the world. It was native to the southeast, but may now be extinct.

Long as a month of Sundays.
☺Note: Due to "blue laws" amusement was once banned on Sundays making it a long day indeed.

Looks greener than gooey gourd guts.
☺Note: The "g" sounds are nearly as funny as "k" sounds.

Looks like Hell with everyone out to lunch.
☺Note: One of the authors all time favorites.

More fun than a sackful of kittens.
☺"Work is more fun than fun."   Noel Coward

More than one way to skin a cat.
☺Note: From the mid-1800. From the phrase, "Like trying to skin a live cat."

No higher than corn and no lower than taters.
☺Meaning: The answer to "How do you want the fence post dug?" About 18' down and 60' up.

Now we're cookin' with gas!
☺Meaning: we're making good progress.

Over yonder at the edge of nothing.
☺Meaning: The edge of the world, "look out you're going to fall off," far.

Pert near, but not plumb.

☺Meaning: just okay, could be "good enough for state work," or how someone is feeling.

Rough as a cob.
☺Note: In earlier times, a corncob was used by some for personal hygiene conducted in the outhouse.

Rougher than a pulp wood truck in a cotton patch.
☺Note: Pulp wood trucks are rough riding and usually noisy.

Scarce as a hen's teeth.
☺Note Researchers from Britain and the US have succeeded in growing teeth in a chicken. Watch for another government funding study on why anyone would want to.

Scarce as deviled eggs after a church picnic.
☺Note: The deviled egg can be seen in recipes as far back as ancient Rome, where they were traditionally served at a first course.

Scattered from Hell to breakfast.
☺From here to East Jesus.

Screamed like a mashed cat.
☺Rather than: Screamed like an 8th lived mashed cat.

Sharper than a mother-in-law's tongue.
☺ Note: Also the name of a houseplant (live imitates botany) which has long sharp leaves in an upright habit.

She didn't say "pea turkey squat".
☺Note: the term "Pea turkey" is a southern-ism meaning "nothing" or "zero".

She was so tall she could hunt geese with a rake.
☺Note: Geese have been recorded at 29,000 feet. That would be a tall drink of water.

She's so deaf, she can't hear a fart in a jug.
☺Note: Why do farts smell? So Deaf people may enjoy them too.

Slapped him like a red-headed stepchild.
☺Note: Red head assumes that neither of the parents had that gene.

Slick as an eel.
☺Fact: Eel blood is toxic to mammals, but both cooking and the digestive process destroy the toxin.

Slick as snot on a goat's glass eye.
☺Note: Goat's glass eye refers to those used in taxidermy.

Slicker than a chased greased hog.
☺Fact: In Minnesota, pig wrestling is a misdemeanor.

Slicker than a minnow's pecker.
☺Fact: Technically fish do not have penises, however some male fish do use tubes, often called "gonopodiums" to internally fertilize eggs.

Slicker than deer guts on a door knob.
☺Note: A very unpleasant way of saying that someone is excessively suave and polished. This can be used in either a derogatory or a neutral sense.

Slicker than otter snot.
☺Meaning: Often used to describe wintery conditions.

Slicker than shit through a tin horn.
☺George S. Patton's famously profane speech to the Third Army "We are going to go through the enemy like shit through a tin horn!"

Slicker than snot and smashed bananas.
☺Note: It turns out that banana skins are, indeed, very slippery. The average coefficient of friction of a banana on linoleum was 0.066. I have no idea what this means. This ain't a science book.

Smaller than a skeeter peter.
☺Fact: "mosquitoes don't have penises - but they can live in doors all year round.

Smaller than a tick turd.
☺Note: Tick and flea "dirt" is feces, which appears on your pet in small, dark clumps.

Smiling like a goat in a brier-patch.
☺Meaning: This phrase is used when somebody is up to no good and trying to hide it.

Smoother than a hairy nipple on wax day.
☺Note: Try to avoid shaving the hairs or using wax treatment, as these may have undesirable results. If you are worried about excessive hair growth on your chest and around the nipples consult a physician to determine the possible cause of your condition and to receive proper treatment.

So deep in jail he'll have to be fed beans with a sling-shot!
☺Note: Jörg Sprave fired a 1-inch steel ball with an arm-braced slingshot, at a speed of 207 feet per second for a world record.

So sore can't touch it with a powder puff.
☺Note: Powder puffs have been made of very fine down feathers, cotton, and fine fleece.

Sober as a judge.
☺Meaning: Not as drunk as a lord.

Squirming like a worm in hot ashes. (Or a hot brick)
☺Meaning: An uncomfortable situation.

Stout as a mule.
☺Fact: Mules have denser muscling than horses due to their donkey parent and therefore can carry more and go farther than a horse of

the same size.

Strong as bear's breath.
☺Note: Bacteria thrive in the mouth of any animal that eats a fat and
meat heavy diet.

Stuck so badly I needed a four wheel drive helicopter to pull my
truck out.
☺Note: If you plan to drive through mud on a regular basis it is wise
to outfit your truck with a winch.

Sweating like a cow in a pasture full of bulls.
☺Note: Cows that are in heat will exhibit telltale signs such as riding,
and being ridden by cattle of either sex.

Tail up and stinger out.
☺Meaning: Ready to go!

Tender as a judge's heart.
☺Fact: The three toughest courtroom judges in 2014 are women.
From Detroit. Go figure

That is just the cat's pajamas.
☺Note: "The cat's pajamas" is first recorded in 1920 as part of the
typical vocabulary of the "flappers."

That kid ain't knee-high to a duck.
☺Note: Ducks don't have knees, instead they have a joint in which
would more accurately be compared to our ankles.

That's lower than quail shit in a wagon rut!
☺Fact: Even after 150 years, there are wagon ruts still observable
from Kansas to California.

The personality of a dishrag.
☺Note: Do not use a dishrag or cloth while cooking because you
will re-contaminate your hands.

There were so many people, you couldn't stir 'em with a stick.
☺Fact: Dharavi slums, Mumbai, India is 770,000 people per square mile, and the most densely populated place on earth.

They could worry the horns off a billy goat.
☺Note: There have been incidents of goats having as many as eight horns – and that is a lot of worrying.

They live so far out they have to pipe in sunshine.
☺Fact: The orange juice company Tropicana created what looks like a sun in the middle of the night in a small Arctic town in Inuvik, Canada

They lived so far out in the country that the sun set between their house and town.
☺Note: This town would have to be no closer than on the moon.

Thick as flies on a dog's back.
☺Fact: Blowfly maggots feed on the dog skin and tissues by producing a special salivary enzyme that is capable of liquefying skin.

Thicker than fiddlers in Hell.
☺Note: From the Charlie Daniels song, "The Devil Went Down to Georgia.".

Tighter than a rat's ass in a keyhole.
☺Note: Rats can fit through small holes because their bodies are long, flexible and cylindrical in shape.

Tighter than a skeeter's ass in a nosedive.
☺Fact: Depending upon the species, mosquitoes can fly up to 1.5 miles per hour.

Weak as dishwater.
☺Meaning: Arousing little interest.

Were closer than two roaches on a bacon bit.
☺Note: Imitation Bacon Bits are made from textured vegetable protein (TVP) - i.e. soy beans.

Whiter than a hound dog's tooth.
☺Note: The hounds-tooth fabric is a duo-tone textile pattern made famous by Bear Bryant.

Wound tighter than a three day clock.
☺Meaning: Tense

Written on the heel.
☺Meaning: It was to be.

You can see it clearer than balls on a tall dog!
☺Note: Makes me want to sing: "do your testes hang low, do they wobble to and fro?"

You can't sling a cat without hitting one.
☺Meaning: "Common." Note: This phrase is probably nautical from "cat-o-nine tails", i.e. a whip.

You look like 10 pounds of smashed assholes in a 5 pound sack.
☺Meaning: Not at all well.

You look like something the cat dragged in and the kittens didn't want.
☺Note: Two teaspoons of whiskey can cause a 5-pound cat to get comatose. Why anyone would waste whiskey on a cat is beyond me.

You're so blind you could miss a crawdad playing cards with Ray Charles.
☺Fact: Ray navigated by the sound of his hard-soled shoes instead of a cane or a dog. He passed in 2004.

You're swinging that driver like a washer woman.

☺Note: When you think of an Irish jig, the song "The Irish Washerwoman" is the tune you're thinking of.

Impoverished: Too poor to paint, too proud to whitewash.

My memories of growing up in the South are happy ones. Those were simpler times when kids had to be called to come back into the house at supper. I had some wealthy classmates in college, but it was not until I experienced Manhattan's wealth disparity did I feel poor.

The South may seem poor by Park Avenue standards, but it is rich in community spirit, self-sufficiency and dignity. More people think they are poor today because the media tells them so. Here are the sayings used in the South to describe those who are less well off.

Ain't got a pot to piss in let alone a window to throw it out of.
☺"We were poor. We were so poor, in my neighborhood the rainbow was in black-and-white." Rodney Dangerfield

As poor as field mice.
☺"If you're in trouble, or hurt or need - go to the poor people. They're the only ones that'll help - the only ones." John Steinbeck

Broke as the Ten Commandments.
☺"The surest way to remain poor is to be an honest man." Napoleon Bonaparte

Don't have a pot to piss in or a window to throw it out of.
☺"The conviction of the rich that the poor are happier is no more foolish than the conviction of the poor that the rich are." Mark Twain

I am so broke I can't buy a flea on a motorcycle jacket.
☺"What I'm saying is we were poor, people; I mean, blues singers would show up at our house when they had writer's block – that's how poor we were." Rich Hall

I couldn't buy a hummingbird on a string for a nickel.
☺"I just filled out my income tax forms. Who says you can't get killed by a blank?" Milton Berle

I couldn't jump over a nickel to save a dime.
☺"Bills travel through the mail at twice the speed of checks."
Steven Wright

If a trip around the world cost a dollar, I couldn't get to the state line.
☺"Money, it turned out, was exactly like sex, you thought of nothing else if you didn't have it and thought of other things if you did." James Baldwin

If I stepped on a worn out dime I could tell you whether it's heads or tails.
☺Rather than: I'm so poor I can't pay attention.

Poor as Job's turkey.
☺Note: A righteous and prosperous man, Job has his faith tested by Satan (with God's permission) and endures all manner of torment, including the loss of his children, his livelihood and his physical health.

So poor he'd have to borrow money to buy water to cry with.
☺"What is the difference between a taxidermist and a tax collector? The taxidermist takes only your skin." Mark Twain

So poor I've got to fart to have a cent.
☺"Acquaintance is a person whom we know well enough to borrow from, but not well enough to lend to." Ambrose Bierce

They ate so many armadillos, grandpa rolls up into a ball when a dog barks.
☺Rather than: We were so poor we had to eat dough for breakfast and sit out in the sun for lunch!

Thick in the middle and poor on both ends.

☺"There are two times in a man's life when he should not speculate: when he can't afford it, and when he can." Mark Twain

Too poor to paint, too proud to whitewash.
☺"I am a poor man, but I have this consolation: I am poor by accident, not by design." Josh Billings

Too poor to pay attention.
☺"When the idle poor become the idle rich, you'll never know just who is who, or which is which." E.Y. Harburg

We were so poor growing up, my brothers had to ride double on a stick horse.
☺"You can be young without money but you can't be old without it." Tennessee Williams

We were so poor I had a tumbleweed as a pet.
☺"We didn't actually overspend our budget. The allocation simply fell short of our expenditure." Keith Davis

We were so poor we had to move every time the rent came due.
☺"I finally know what distinguishes man from other beasts: financial worries." Jules Renard

We were so poor we had to use a 'possum as a yard dog.
☺"One of the strangest things about life is that the poor, who need money the most, are the very ones who never have it." Finley Peter Dunne

We were so poor we had to use a possum as a yard dog.
☺Note: Some people have kept opossums as pets and enjoyed their company very much. Usually the best pets are those rescued when very young.

Insults: Can't never could.

In the 19th Century, New Orleans had the distinction of having more duels than any other American city. Creoles were expert swordsmen and duels were sometimes provoked by young men who delighted in any opportunity to exhibit their art. Duels were fought by rivals for a lady, a politics, or even difference of opinion regarding an opera.

Legend has it that a European scientist had to fight a duel because he insulted the Mississippi River in the presence of a Creole. The scientist had sneered at the Mississippi, saying it was, "but a tiny rill compared to the great rivers of Europe." For this the European received a slashed cheek from the Creole's sword.

Unfortunately, today's duels are fought with words. Southerners are as expert in wordplay as they once were in sword play. In case you get challenged due to the favors of a lady, politics, or college football, here are the insults you will need to defend yourself.

Almost as smart as people say he thinks he is.
☺"The problem with the world is that the intelligent people are full of doubts, while the stupid ones are full of confidence." Charles Bukowski

Can't never could.
☺Note: This is the male version of "aww Hell no".

Give me a fly-snapper and I'll help you kill it.
☺Note: Reserved for situation where a woman you don't like well is sporting an outrageous hairdo or hat.

I've stepped over better than you looking for a place to piss.
☺Rather than: Asshole casserole

If I want your opinion I will unscrew the top of your head and dip it out.

☺Rather than: You shut your mouth when you're talking to me.

If stupid could fly, you'd be a jet.

☺Rather than: I don't think you act stupid, I'm sure it's the real thing.

If a gnat had your brain it would fly backwards.

☺Note: Gnats spend most of their short lives laying eggs. To trap them, mix a half cup of vinegar and a tablespoon of Dawn dish detergent in a bowl.

If I had a dog as ugly as you, I'd shave his butt and make him walk backwards.

☺Fact: Most animals can walk backwards, but not kangaroos. This isn't the only reason not to do it however.

If you had any brains you would be dangerous.

☺Fact: Only 2% of the world's population has an IQ of 130 or higher.

When you die you're gonna have to rise up to find Hell.

☺Rather than: Sometimes the first step to forgiveness, is realizing the other person was born an idiot.

You are going to Hell on a scholarship.

☺Note: Possibly today it could be: "You're going to college on student loans."

You know I wouldn't shit you. You're my favorite turd.

☺"I went to the turd museum, they've got some great shit in there. Some of that crap is worth a lot of money". Steve Martin

You now as much about that as a hog knows about Sunday.

☺Rather than: Stupidity comes in all shapes and sizes. Some of them even look like people.

You shouldn't be hunting anything smarter than you.

☺Fact: Chimpanzees are thought to be the most intelligent animals with IQs in the mid-80s.

<u>You smell like you want to be left alone.</u>
☺Fact: If people has a dog's sense of smell, we could tell what a person ate last night, and the brand of toilet paper they use and if they need Wipees.

<u>Your momma should have killed you and sold the milk.</u>
☺Rather than: Too many freaks, not enough circuses.

<u>Your truck couldn't pull a fat baby off a tricycle.</u>
☺Rather than: Do you jump start your Toyota Prius with your phone?

Intoxicated: Drunker than a bicycle.

It's not that Southerners drink more, it's just more frequent. As someone pointed out, when it's 98 degrees outside, a cold beer is like finding a winning lottery ticket. Cocktails in the South are served before supper (dinner), not under the muted neon glare of the ESPN hockey channel. If you do manage to "over do", there are sayings for intoxicated, just not a lot of them.

Drunker than a bicycle.
☺Also: Drunker than a duck.

He was drunker than a skunk.
☺"I got so drunk one night I woke up in a chalk outline." Tim Northern

He was drunker than Cooter Brown on the 4th of July.
☺Note: Legend says that Cooter stayed drunk during the entire Civil War to avoid fighting.

He's so drunk he couldn't hit the floor with his hat.
☺Rather than: Why is there so much blood in my alcohol system?

Higher than a Georgia pine.
☺"You are not drunk if you can lie on the floor without holding on." Dean Martin

Three sheets in the wind.
☺Rather than: I've got to sit down and work out where I stand.

Tore up from the floor up.
☺Rather than: I don't have a drinking problem – as long as I am drinking – no problem.

Lazy: He follows the shade around the house.

I have a friend who has a dog and a cat. Sometimes the dog wants to sleep in the bedroom, sometimes the dog wants to sleep outside the bedroom. But, the dog never decides until my friend is all settled in bed. Once the dog decides where he's sleeping, my friend uses a laser pointer to shine on the door so that the cat paws it closed. It has now become so routine that the cat wait by the door at bedtime.

Impressive! Here are the ways to describe a lazy dog in the South.

Born in the middle of the week and looking both ways for Sunday.
☺"A loafer always has the correct time." Frank Hubbard

Dead flies wouldn't fall off of him.
☺Note: Hard work has a future payoff. - Laziness pays off now.

Follows the shade around the house.
☺ Consciousness: that annoying time between naps.

He moves like the lice is falling off him.
☺Fact: The mitochondrial DNA of lice is used to determine migration patterns of ancient humans.

He wouldn't hit a lick with a snake.
☺Meaning: He wouldn't "lick" or hit a snake if it was right by him.

He wouldn't say "shit" if he had a mouthful of it.
☺Fact: Centuries ago, physicians tasted their patients' feces, to better judge their state and condition.

He wouldn't take time to say "shit" if he had a mouthful of it.
☺"I should have suspected my husband was lazy; on our wedding day, his mother told me: 'I'm not losing a son; I'm gaining a couch.'"
Phyllis Diller

He's got molasses in his britches.
☺Note: Lazy people are always anxious to be doing something.

He's so lazy he calls the dog inside to see if it's raining.
☺"Blame is just a lazy person's way of making sense of chaos."
Douglas Coupland

Sitting there like a wart on a frog.
☺Note: The bumps and the lumps you see on the skin of some amphibians (usually toads) are glands filled with foul-tasting poison.

So lazy he wouldn't work in a pie factory as a taster.
☺Note: The best key lime pie can be found at Key West Key Lime Pie Co. It's in Key West of course; check their website for openings.

That boy wouldn't work in a pie factory, afraid he'd get full and have to quit.
☺ If you're too lazy to start anything, you may get a reputation for patience

Luck: Both Kinds.

In 2001 I joined Cantor Fitzgerald in the North Tower, 105th floor of the World Trade Center. For my entire career I was at my desk by 7AM, however just prior to Sept. 11, the chairman of Cantor Fitzgerald informed me that he wanted me to work his hours. This would mean starting at roughly 9AM and staying into the evening. September 11. 2001 was to be the first day I would work that schedule. I was parking my car when the first plane hit my office, but I witnessed the second plane.

Luck is often a double edged sword. Here are the Southern sayings for both kinds of luck.

A wing and a prayer.
☺Also: All's well that ends.

Even a blind hog finds an acorn every once in a while.
☺Rather than: Even a blind squirrel can find a nut.

Good Luck says, "Open your mouth and shut your eyes."
☺Fact: Journal of Sensory Studies, has determined that the seeing does actually change the perceived flavors of food.

He's riding the gravy train with biscuit wheels.
☺Meaning: He has been very lucky up to now.

I could fall into a barrel of teats and come out sucking my thumb; He could sit on the fence and the birds would feed him.
☺"I think we consider too much the good luck of the early bird and not enough the bad luck of the early worm." Franklin D. Roosevelt

If he fell into an outhouse he'd come up smelling like a rose.
☺Never bet on a loser because you think his luck is bound to change.

It doesn't take a prophet to predict bad luck.
☺"We must believe in luck; for how else can we explain the success of those we don't like." Jean Cocteau

The sun don't shine on the same dog's tail all the time.
☺"As long as we are lucky we attribute it to our smartness; our bad luck we give the gods credit for." Josh Billings

You must not be holding your mouth right. (Or living your life right)
☺Note: A golf match is a test of your skill against your opponents' luck.

Meals: So good you'll want to slap granny.

Southern cooking styles and flavors can vary greatly by region. The closer to the coastal area, the stronger the influence of West African methods and spices. The mountainous areas did not have slaves, so that the food and dialect is distinct. BBQ in Texas is very different than Alabama. Louisiana is a more French than African.

Southern food defines the culture, and is taken very seriously by the cooks. Accordingly there are many sayings to describe the food of the South.

Anything with a beak and a wing is a beautiful thing.
☺Meaning: God bless the "yard bird."

Ate that chicken until it was slick as a ribbon.
☺Meaning: That you are all the meat, skin, and sinew until the chicken bone was slick.

Barely fit to eat.
☺Meaning: It's so good I don't want to pass it around the table.

Coffee so strong it'll walk into your cup.
☺Note: To make better strong coffee, buy whole beans and grind it fresh and fine.

Coffee's strong enough to float an iron wedge.
☺Note: Start with a ratio of one rounded tablespoon of coffee grounds per eight ounces of water. Gradually increase grinds in ½ tablespoon increments until you find the perfect ratio for your taste.

Eating the gospel bird.
☺Note: Many families have chicken dinner on Sunday right after church.

Full as a tick on a fat frisky pup.
☺Note: Full as a tick on Chris Christie, the Governor of New Jersey and round mound of sound.

Good as a cold collard sandwich.
☺Meaning: Not good. However, there are warm varieties I would be tempted by.

Granny cooked enough supper to feed Pharaoh's army.
☺Note: Locally if there was a large military camp, during WW2 for example, the commanding officer would be used. In Memphis it was "Enough to feed Cox's army."

I am so hungry I can see biscuits walking on crutches!
☺Note: Originally it was: "I'm so hungry I could see a bow-legged biscuit walk a crooked mile."

I am so hungry I could eat the ass end out of a rag doll.
☺Rather than: I could eat a horse and chase the jockey

I could eat the north end of a south-bound goat.
☺Note: Goat Roasts are common in the some parts of the South. Goats are 3% fat, and much leaner than beef (18%) or even turkey (5%) and chicken (7%).

I'd eat the balls off a low flying duck!
☺Fact: Ducks must ingest than 300 invertebrates an hour for eight hours to produce enough energy for one egg.

I'm so hungry I could eat a frozen dog!
☺Fact: Only northern dog breeds like huskies and malamutes are allowed in the Iditarod Race. The rule was adopted in the early 1990s after musher John Suter entered the 1988 competition with standard European poodles- which promptly froze.

I'm so hungry my belly button is sticking out of my butt.
☺Fact: Most "outies" are nothing more than extra scar tissue.

Rarely are they caused by an umbilical hernia, and they normally heal within a year.

I'm so hungry, every time I swallow my asshole says thank you.
☺Fact: Michel Lotito ate an entire Cessna 150 aircraft over a one year period.

I'm as hungry as a tick on a turnip.
☺Fact: Adult stage deer ticks become active every year after the first frost. They're not killed by freezing temperatures, and while other ticks enter a feeding pause as day-lengths get shorter, deer ticks will be active any winter day that the ground is not snow-covered or frozen.

I'm so hungry I'm fartin' cobwebs.
☺Fact: A newly discovered species of spider from Madagascar spins some of the largest webs in the world - about 9 feet in diameter.

I'm so hungry my backbone is snapping at my belt buckle.
☺Rather than: I am so hungry I could eat a beer battered monkey.

I'm so hungry my belly thinks my throat's been cut.
☺Rather than: I could eat a baby's arse through a wicker chair

I hope I remembered my space panties.
☺Rather than: I need my fat pants.

I'm hungry enough to eat a pigtail sandwich.
☺Note: Pigtails are finding new fans in the north, but in the South everything put the "oink" is eaten.

I've seen animals hurt worse than that get well.
☺Meaning: The steak was very rare.

If it can't be cooked with bacon grease, it ain't worth making, let alone eating.
☺Note: Bacon grease for anything you'd use butter for and it lasts

indefinitely.

If you go away clean you ain't eating it right.
☺Note: Often said while eating BBQ – that is pork, slow cooked. Maybe beef.

It was so good it would have brought tears to a glass eye.
☺Note: Artificial eyes are usually German made and like toys, they were made by families of peasant artisans living in the Black Forest or other remote regions.

It will make your tongue slap your brains out.
☺Meaning: It's good,

It'll make your liver quiver and your bladder splatter.
☺Note: The phrase was also used to introduce James Brown.

Knock the horns off, wipe its ass, and drag it in.
☺Meaning: You'd like it raw, not rare.

My mouth is dry enough to spin cotton.
☺Note: I don't know why I'm so thirsty today, I drank a lot last night.

Put on the dog.
☺Meaning: To put out the best of everything for a meal.

So bad it would snatch the taste right out of her mouth.
☺"My cooking is so bad my kids thought Thanksgiving was to commemorate Pearl Harbor." Phyllis Diller

So good it'll make your tongue jump out and lick the eyebrows right off your head.
☺Fact: Californian Nick Stoeberl holds the record for the world's longest tongue at 4 inches.

Tastes so good it makes you want to slap your grandma.
☺Meaning: It was really good.

That BBQ is tangier than my brother's cutoffs.
☺Meaning: "Tangy" may also refer to "rancid" in an ironic twist.

That coffee is too thick to drink and too thin to plow.
☺'Death Wish Coffee' of NYC comes with a health warning (as well as a money back guarantee) if it isn't the strongest coffee you've ever had.

That is cooked to a turn!
☺Meaning: Done just right.

That ran through me like a dose of salts.
☺Note: "Salts" are Epsom Salt and used as a laxative to relieve occasional constipation.

The coffee has been saucered and blowed.
☺Meaning: The coffee is ready to enjoy.

This will make your tongue slap your brains out.
☺"You don't need a silver fork to eat good food."   Paul Prudhomme

Momma Said: Don't be ugly.

A wary Southern child's first clue that something was amiss is found in these sayings. Body language clues are important to key off. For instance, if your mother was busy at the kitchen sink and did a parade ground heel-snap, with a wooden spoon in one hand....well it's best to confess now. Even in that, there is a lot of love in this advice, so "get your butt off your shoulders", and pay attention.

A body can't get a minute's peace in this house.
☺Meaning: It is cocktail hour yet? It's 5 o'clock somewhere.

A hard head makes a soft behind.
☺"Give me a smart idiot over a stupid genius any day." Samuel Goldwyn

A little bird told me.
☺Note: Answer to "How did you know I did that?"

Act like you got some raisin'.
☺ Also heard: Act like you're somebody.

Better not let your shirt tail touch your back until you get it done.
☺Meaning: Don't stop until you finish the job.

Better tend to your own knittin'.
☺Meaning: Mind you own business.

Bless your heart
☺Meaning: This phrase could mean nothing at all, to: "you are a freakin' idiot", and everything in between.

Bumper shoot.
☺Note: Another word for umbrella. Word umbrella comes from the Latin word "umbros" which means shade or shadow.

Butter my butt and call me a biscuit!
☺Also: Paint me green and call me a cucumber.

Close the door, you're letting the flies out.
☺Fact: Vanilla scents and cloves keeps flies away.

Don't be ugly to your sister.
☺Meaning: Be nice.

Don't get your cows running.
☺Meaning: Relax.

Don't look at me in that tone of voice.
☺Meaning: Ironic version of, "Don't give me the fish eye."

Don't monkey with that.
☺Meaning: Put that down. Frequently heard at the grocery store
checkout late.

Don't sass back.
☺Note: The term "sass" has been around since the mid-1800s and
means: Impertinent, disrespectful speech; back talk.

Don't worry about closing the barn door now once the cows got out.
☺Meaning: It's too late to worry about that now.

Don't worry that.
☺Meaning: Leave it be.

Don't you make eyes at me.
☺Meaning: Don't look at me in that tone of look.

Don't you stand there looking at me like a dying bull in a hailstorm!
☺Meaning: Move your butt!

Dug in like an Appalachian tick.

☺Note: Many outdoors-men recommended Lyme blood tests after hiking or camping.

Faint of heart never won fair maiden.
☺Meaning: Nothing ventured, nothing gained.

Get back on your lily pad.
☺Meaning: This conversation doesn't concern you.

Get your butt off your shoulders!
☺Rather than: Get your head out of your ass.

Getting too big for your britches.
☺Meaning: I am old enough to know you don't know everything.

Go after them like a biting sow!
☺Note: This saying was first heard during the Civil War.

Go cut me a switch – and if it's not to my liking I will cut one for you.
☺Meaning: a young, green switch.

Go cut me a switch.
☺Meaning: It's fanny whooping time.

Go on and run - y'all gotta come home sometime.
☺Meaning: It's fanny whooping time when you come back.

God blessed the dirt; the dirt will not hurt, put it in your mouth and let it work.
☺Note: Eating clay or Pica is common in some areas and has been found to sooth stomach disorders. Hippocrates, the 5th-century BC Greek physician, noted that pregnant women often had cravings for earth or charcoal.

Has the cat got your tongue?
☺Meaning: Answer me before I get a switch.

Have clean drawers on if you're going somewhere - you may get in a car accident.
☺Fact: 1 in 8 men wear their underwear up to 3 times before washing.

He buttered his britches.
☺Meaning: Someone needs a diaper change.

Hold your horses.
☺Meaning: Relax for a moment. Note: Origins of the phrase, dating back to usage in Ancient Greece

I am fixin' to lose my religion.
☺Meaning: I have run out of patience.

If I tell you a rooster can pull a wagon, hitch'em up.
☺Meaning: I know what I'm talking about.

I brought you into this world I'll take you out.
☺Note: This statement might also be added: "It makes no difference to me because I will just make another one that looks just like you." Whoa!

I didn't just fall off the turnip truck.
☺Also heard: I didn't just ride in on a load of pumpkins.

I got one nerve left and you are jumping all over it.
☺Fact: According to Neurogenetics at the University of Tennessee Health Science Center, the human body has 95 to 100 billion nerve cells.

I love you like a bushel and a peck, and a hug around your neck.
☺Note: One (1) US peck = 1/4 of a US bushel = 2 US dry gallons.

I love you so much I could eat you up blood raw with no salt!
☺Fact: Many cultures consume blood in the form of blood sausage,

as a thickener, in a cured salted form, or in a blood soup.

I see Christmas!
☺Meaning: I see your snow-white underwear.

I would rather go to a shit slinging than be seen wearing something like that.
☺Meaning: Take that off.

I'll knock you into the middle of next week looking both ways for Sunday!
☺Meaning: I'm not waiting for the switch.

I'll slap a knot on your head it will take a bulldozer to smooth out.
☺Note from author: This makes my head hurt just reading it.

I'm fixin' to put some nickel knots on your head.
☺Note: Nickels are 75 percent copper and 25 percent nickel. When metal prices spiked in 2006, Nickels were worth 7 cents.

I'm gonna slap you so hard when you quit rollin' your clothes will be outta style.
☺Note: For men that would be about 25 years. For women, 5 years tops.

I'm gonna jerk you bald!
☺Fact: Trichotillomania is a compulsive disorder which causes people to pull their hair out. It affects 4 percent of the population. It is more likely to occur in women than in men.

If you can go out on Saturday night you can go to church on Sunday morning.
☺Meaning: If you're going to dance, you've got to pay the piper.

If you fall out of that tree and break your leg don't come running to me.
☺"Always be sincere, even when you don't mean it." Irene Peter

If you keep an aspirin between your legs you cannot get pregnant.
☺Meaning: Keep your legs closed.

If you mess with crap, you get crap on you.
☺Meaning: Your friends are a reflection of you.

If you're going to be a turd go lay in the yard.
☺Note: No explanation needed - this is one my favorites.

If you're gonna be stupid, you better be tough.
☺"Critics should find meaningful work."   John Grisham

If your jobs are small and your rewards seem few, remember the mighty oak was once a nut like you.
☺Note: From the adage:" Mighty oaks from little acorns grow"

Instead of saying "hey", save it - you might marry a jackass one day.
☺Meaning: Don't say "hey", say "hello."

Is this what you wanna be doing when Jesus comes back?
☺Meaning: Lock the door next time and give me that girlie magazine.

It's time to get ready for Mrs. White's party.
☺Meaning: Refers to white bed linens: it's bed time.

It's gonna take a rusty corncob to get this dirt off you.
☺Note: Corn cobs were used to scour things clean.

Just sit there and sip your tea.
☺Meaning: Mind your own affairs.

Keep it up and you're gonna be sitting at the right foot of the Devil.
☺Note: King James Bible Romans 16:20. And the God of peace shall bruise Satan under your feet shortly.

Kids could break a second-hand anvil with a turkey feather.
☺Note: Self-explanatory if you have kids. If you don't have kids, believe the rest of us on this.

Let the hair go with the hide.
☺Rather than: What will be will be.

Little pictures have big ears.
☺Meaning: Whatever parents say at breakfast will be in the school paper by homeroom.

Make sure you wash where the Yankee shot you.
☺Meaning: Wash your navel.

Me 'n you are about to have a "come to Jesus" meeting.
☺Rather than: You better straighten up and fly right.

Monkey see monkey do.
☺Note: The saying is probably from the folklore of Mali, West Africa and first appeared in the US around 1920.

No matter where you go, there you are.
☺Note: Famous quote also in the cult classic "Buckaroo Banzai."

Noisy enough to wake the dead.
☺Rather than: Keep it to a dull roar please.

Nothing is wasted around here, we eat everything from the snooter to the tooter.
☺Note: If you've eaten sausage, or scrapple, you have eaten everything but the "oink."

Pretty is as pretty does.
☺Meaning: Good character and behavior are more important than good looks.

Put on your big boy britches.

☺Meaning: Man up man.

Quit acting like your daddy's people.
☺"I married your mother because I wanted children, imagine my disappointment when you came along." Groucho Marx

Quit going around your ass to get to your elbow.
☺Meaning: Get on with it.

Raise that window down.
☺Note: The ironic version of "close that window."

Raising kids is like being pecked to death by a chicken.
☺Note: Like Chinese Water Torture, a steady stream of small, minor nuisances build up over time to the point where you tear off your clothes and run down the street.

Stop jumping around like piss-ants on a hot griddle.
☺Meaning: Settle down.

Stop that crying before I give you something to cry about.
☺Note: This statement will usually get the silence you've craved.

Stubborn like a billy goat: hard head and stinking butt.
☺Note: A goat's rectangular pupil allows them to see 320 degrees and better at night. You're not sneaking up on one.

Tell the truth and shame the Devil.
☺Meaning: Tell the truth even though you have may have strong reasons for concealing it.

That boy has a lot of quit in him.
☺My father was a quitter, my grandfather was a quitter, I was raised to give up. It's one of the few things I do well." Jason Alexander

That boy is a poster child for birth control.
☺Meaning: Darwin's law being broken,

That lie is gonna split Hell right open.
☺Meaning: That was a good lie even by profession standards. Thought about running for office?

That's not sweet.
☺Meaning: A version of "Don't be ugly."

That's tacky.
☺Meaning: You're not leaving the house in that, or don't say that word again.

That's your red wagon to pull.
☺Meaning: That is your problem. Note: The Radio Flyer has been made since 1923.

The higher a monkey climbs the more he shows his ass.
☺Note: West African saying that politicians haven't taken heed.

The Lord greased your butt and slid you down a rainbow.
☺Answer to the question, "Where did I come from?"

The proof is in the pudding.
☺Note: The phrase originally was "The proof of the pudding is in the eating."

There's a dead cat on the line.
☺Meaning: I don't believe you.

This ain't the Governor's ball you're going to.
☺Meaning: You're taking too long to get ready.

Two buzzards bumped butts and you fell out.
☺Note: Another good answer to the question, "Where do babies come from?"

Well, now, little lady.

☺Note: This phrase is how many "Come to Jesus" meetings begin.

What in the Sam Hill is going on?
☺Note: Sam Hill is one of many euphemisms for 'hell'.

Why, bless your little pea-pickin' heart.
☺Note: "Pea-pickin' was a catchphrase of Tennessee Ernie Ford. He was noted for his rich bass-baritone voice and down-home humor as well as the recordings of "The Shotgun Boogie" and "Sixteen Tons".

You are acting like a cat's aunt Jane.
☺Meaning: You are acting like a brat.

You are stubborn as a blue-nosed mule.
☺Note: Old-timers used to call a dark muzzled mule "blue nosed".

You are wild as a March hare.
☺Note: Rabbits will behave strangely throughout the breeding season. This odd behavior includes boxing at other hares, jumping vertically for seemingly no reason and generally displaying abnormal behavior.

You can just get glad in the same britches you got mad in.
☺Meaning: Stop pouting.

You can't fool God and you can't fool me!
☺Note: A turn pf phrase from F. Scott Fitzgerald's The Great Gatsby, "You may fool me, but you can't fool God!" - Doctor T. J. Eckleburg.

You kids are standing around the kitchen like buzzards on a gut wagon.
☺Note: This phrase was used several times on the TV series "ALF".

You make my butt want to dip snuff.
☺Note: Snuff is used by placing a lump or "dip" of tobacco between the lip and the gum.

You're eating like a field hand.
☺Meaning: Your elbows are on the table, you're gobbling, and other infractions.

You're going to wool that baby to death.
☺Note: "Wooling" is to be overly attentive.

You're gonna have old and new-monia dressed like that!
☺Note: "Monia" is a play on word with "pneumonia."

You're gonna mess with me and fall back in it!
☺Meaning: I will kick the $hit out of you.

You're looking at me like cow looking at a new gate.
☺Meaning: That you are looking to take advantage.

You're the spitting image of your mother/father.
☺Note: The term "spit" and "splitting" is deriving from the two matching parts of a split plank of wood used to make a string instrument.

Your barn door's open and the mule is trying to run.
☺Meaning: Your purpose in life is out. Please check your zipper.

Your face is gonna freeze like that.
☺Meaning: Don't make ugly faces, including crossing your eyes. Note: Although crossing your eyes for an extended period of time might cause a temporary strain on your eye muscles, no medical evidence suggests that they would stick that way.

Your momma wasn't a glass blower.
☺Meaning: Don't stand there, I can't see TV. Note: You'll use this a hundred times, as all kids think they are made of glass.

In between the devil and the deep blue sea.
☺Note: The "devil" was a name for the longest seam of a wooden ship, which often had to be caulked while in transit.

Nervous: Like a cat on a hot tin roof.

My son pitched in baseball. I never missed a game, but was often so nervous that I would peek around the dugout with only one eye open to watch. My son, however, was Mr. Cool. It didn't matter if bases were loaded with a full count. He was smiling. His strategy? Think of someone that makes you smile. For my son, it was my dad, his grandfather.

Humor is a guaranteed way to relieve stress. Here are funny Southernisms to help.

Like a frog on the freeway with a busted jumper.
☺Note: "Frogger", circa 1981, is regarded as a classic from the golden age of video arcade.

Like a long tail cat in a room full of rocking chairs.
☺Facts: Tail injuries can cause permanent nerve damage, even though the spinal cord doesn't reach into the tail.

Like a porcupine in a balloon factory.
☺Also with an ironic twist: Like a balloon in a porcupine factory.

Like a spring lizard in a hen-house.
☺Note: Chickens will eat anything they can over power.

My nuts are drawn up so tight you couldn't reach them with knitting needles.
☺Fact: 88.7% of Darwin Award winners were guys. Note: The award recognizes individuals who have supposedly contributed to human evolution by selecting themselves out of the gene pool via death or sterilization by their own actions.

Nervous as a bear caught with his head in the hive.
☺Note: Bears do get stung, they just "bear the pain."

Nervous as a cow with a bucktooth calf.
☺Note: Apparently a buck tooth cow says, "moof."

Nervous as a whore in church.
☺Fact: In the formative years of the United States, prostitution was widely legal. Prostitution was made illegal in almost all states between 1910 and 1915 largely due to the influence of the Woman's Christian Temperance Union.

That would twist the back of your crotch out.
☺Note: In the Civil War, CSA privates were often spotted due to their pants seats being completely wore out.

Wound tighter than a new girdle.
☺Note: In the early 1900s, the "mono-bosom" was a popular look for women. Their breasts were hoisted and supported in such a way to appear as though they had one large bosom.

You couldn't drive a toothpick up my butt with a sledgehammer.
☺Meaning: Very nervous, thank God. Otherwise it would be very painful.

No: I'd rather sandpaper a bobcat's ass in a phone booth.

Why say "no", when you paint an image of no. Southern culture shares with England the love of work play. If in London, don't be surprised if instead of "no", the speaker says something like, "I've got trouble and strife." Southern sayings for "no" are much easier to fathom, here are the ones to know.

Does a chicken have lips?
☺Rather than: Do pigs fly?

Hard sayin' not knowin'.
☺Meaning: Don't press the issue.

I'd rather be beat with a sack of wet catfish.
☺Note: The Gafftopsail Catfish is found in the waters of the western central Atlantic Ocean, as well as the Gulf of Mexico and Caribbean. It has long, venomous spines. A sack of them would hurt quite a bit I would imagine.

I'd rather be in Hell with a broken back.
☺Note: Also used by James Cagney in the movie: "One, Two, Three."

I'd rather have a tick in my navel.
☺Note: On humans, ticks prefer behind the knees, between the legs, under the arms and sometimes in the belly button.

I'd rather jump barefoot off a 6-foot step ladder into a 5 gallon bucket full of porcupines.
☺Fact: The word "porcupine" comes from the middle or old French word "porcespin", which means spiny pig.

I'd rather sandpaper a bobcat's ass in a phone booth.

☺Fact: Bobcat prefer rabbits, but will take anything from insects, to fowl, rodents, and deer.

I'd rather stare at the Sun with binoculars.
☺Fact: It would take less than a second to blind you, even without the binoculars.

I'll be dipped in bacon fat before I do that.
☺Fact: Bacon is an excellent source of choline, which helps improve intelligence and memory; as well as fight Alzheimer's.

I'll pay you when my coon gets fat.
☺Note: Raccoons don't make good pets, so this would mean "no" or "never."

I'm near about past going.
☺Meaning: I'm not going.

In a pig's eye.
☺Note: Since a pig's eye is small, so are the chances of "yes".

Like a kerosene cat in Hell with gasoline drawers on.
☺Meaning: No chance.

That dog won't hunt.
☺Also: That cat won't flush.

That is too much pumpkin for a nickel.
☺Meaning: It is more trouble than it's worth.

That will go over go over like a pregnant pole-vaulter.
☺Rather than: That will go over like a lead Zepplin.

That's a gracious plenty.
☺Meaning: "Stop" or "no".

You might as well shove your money up a wolf's ass and watch him

<u>run over the hill.</u>
☺"There is much pleasure to be gained from useless knowledge."
Bertrand Russell

Odors: It could knock a buzzard off a gut wagon.

Hopefully you'll take advantage of the outdoors in the South. With the outdoors comes orders and Mother Nature is a smelly lady. Here are the Southernisms you need to be acquainted with the sporting life.

Gag a maggot!
☺Fact: Maggots have been used in the treatment of non-healing wounds.

He was farting like a pack mule.
☺Note: Mules with full bellies are less inclined to wander and also more content in camp. They will also be more gassy.

It smelled worse than a dead skunk that just crawled out of another dead skunk's ass.
☺Fact: A skunk can spray up to 10 feet in distance.

It smells like tomcats fighting.
☺Fact: Male cat urine is full of testosterone, signaling to nearby males to stay away and letting females know there's romance nearby.

Stronger than ten acres of garlic.
☺Fact: Garlic field are pungent, but the plants keep mosquitoes away.

That smells like the shithouse door on a shrimp boat.
☺Fact: Cruise ships may dump untreated sewage from toilets once the ships are three miles from shore.

That stinks so bad it could knock a buzzard off a gut wagon.
☺Fact: Turkey vultures can pick out carrion smells from more than a mile away.

That stinks to high heaven.

☺Fact: The speed of smell is about 1/3rd of the average speed of the molecules of oxygen in the air.

That would gag a maggot on a gut wagon.
☺Fact: Most of a slaughtered farm animal cannot be transformed into edible flesh -about 60% is inedible.

Plumpish: It takes two dogs to bark at her.

The better the food in your state, the more plump you're likely to be. My home state of Mississippi is the most obese in the country by some polls. Baby-boomers are more likely to be porcine as are lower income folks. I'd take these polls with a grain of salt (on catfish and hush-puppies please) as some of the pollsters are finding that Southerners are just more honest about their weight than other states.

It's all too easy to ignore the consequence of that second helping of blackberry cobbler. Here are the phrases you'll be hearing at the beach to help you resist.

<u>Fat people are harder to kidnap.</u>
☺Rather than: When he joined Overeaters Anonymous and they make him a chapter.

<u>Fatter than the town dog.</u>
☺Note: Many towns had a dog that belong to no one and everyone.

<u>He didn't get a round mouth by eating square meals.</u>
☺Rather than: He is so fat… his shadow weighs 12 pounds.

<u>He's digging his grave with his spoon.</u>
☺"When it comes to eating, you can sometimes help yourself more by helping yourself less." Richard Armour

<u>He's got Dunlap's disease - his belly done lapped over his belt.</u>
☺Rather than: A waist is a terrible thing to mind.

<u>He's got the furniture disease.</u>
☺ Meaning: His chest has fallen into his drawers.

<u>His ass must be hungry - it's trying to eat his pants.</u>
☺Rather than: He's so big, it takes two men and a boy just to look at

him.

If she were an inch taller she'd be round.
☺"I was never over-weight, just under-tall; the correct height for my weight at the moment is seven feet ten and a half inches." Brendan Grace

If somebody told her to "haul ass," she'd have to make two trips.
☺Rather than: I keep trying to lose weight… but it keeps finding me.

It takes two dogs to bark at her.
☺Rather than: At the zoo, the elephants throw peanuts at her.

Piggy Wiggly hires a rodeo clown to distract her when grocery shopping.
☺Rather than: Her favorite meal is seconds.

She's spread out like a cold supper.
☺"If you can't tell the difference between a spoon and a ladle, then you're fat." Demetri Martin

They stepped up on the scale to be weighed, it said "To be continued."
☺ Rather than: He is so fat… his driver's license says, "picture continued on other side."

Proverbs: A gallant retreat is better than a bad stand.

Both the Southern dialect and idioms are largely based on late Elizabethan English and the languages of West Africa. Proverbs are the capsules of condensed wisdom, values and beliefs of the culture. In the South, these proverbs are a legacy passed down from generation to the next. Like dialect, proverbs have great influence on the fabric of a culture because they are absorbed at an early age. Here are many of the proverbs Southerners heard since they were "knee high to a duck."

A blacksnake knows the way to the hen's nest.
☺Meaning: A dishonest person will keep at it until caught.

A blind horse doesn't fall when he follows the bit.
☺Meaning: Following instructions and everything will be fine.

A blind mule ain't afraid of darkness.
☺Meaning: What haven't experienced you are not afraid of.

A bull without horns can still smart.
☺Meaning: Something or somebody that is not quite what they used to be can still be dangerous – that that first wife / husband.

A bumblebee is faster than a John Deere tractor.
☺Meaning: If you run over a nest in a tractor, jump off and start running.

A cat can have kittens in an oven, but that don't make 'em biscuits.
☺Also: Going to church doesn't make you a hymnal.

A crooked cornstalk can still have a straight ear.
☺Rather than: One bad apple doesn't ruin the whole bunch.

A full purse ain't half as good as an empty one is bad.

☺Rather than: It's better than nothing.

A gallant retreat is better than a bad stand.
☺"Never confuse a single defeat with a final defeat." F. Scott Fitzgerald

A good farmer stays acquainted with daybreak.
☺"Early to bed, and early to rise, makes a man healthy, wealthy and wise." Ben Franklin.

A guilty dog barks the loudest.
☺"The lady doth protest too much, methinks," Hamlet by William Shakespeare.

A guilty fox hunts his own hole.
☺Meaning: To return to the scene of the crime.

A hole in your britches lets in a heap of uneasiness.
☺"Few things in life are more embarrassing than the necessity of having to inform an old friend that you have just got engaged to his fiancée." W.C. Fields

A miss is as good as a mile.
☺Meaning: A close miss is as bad as a wide miss - they are both misses.

A mule can be tame at one end and wild at the other.
☺Note: Mules are more intelligent that horse or donkeys. They are also highly curious in nature and generally do follow dangerous paths.

A new broom sweeps clean, but an old one knows where the dirt is.
☺"Immature love says: 'I love you because I need you.' Mature love says 'I need you because I love you.' Erich Fromm

A one-eyed mule can't be handled on the blind side.
☺Note: A mule can carry "dead weight" up to 20% of its body

weight.

A pig has enough arithmetic to take the shortest cut through a thicket.
☺Note: Pigs are highly intelligent, in one study they even put their toys away before bedtime – which makes them smarter than my sons.

A pullet can't roost too high for an owl.
☺Note: A pullet is a young chicken, usually is less than a year old.

A rabbit knows a fox track same as a hound does.
☺Meaning: A rabbit has more at stake than the hound, but as much as the fox.

A sharp ax is better than big muscle.
☺Meaning: Use your head, not your back.

A sleepy fisherman totes a light load home.
☺Fish are most active in morning and evening, but in a waxing moon you'll catch less. FYI.

A sore back mule is a poor hand at guessing the weight of a sack of meal.
☺Meaning: Don't overload you mule or truck.

A whistling woman and a crowing hen never come to a very good end.
☺Meaning: Don't brag.

A wink is as good as a nod to a blind horse.
☺Meaning: Some people just can't take a hint.

A wink is as good as a nod, to a blind horse.
☺Meaning: Some people can't take a hint.

A worm is the only animal that can't fall down.
☺Meaning: Some people are already worm-low.

Ain't no point in beatin' a dead horse – but then it can't hurt either.
☺Rather than: It's like putting gas into a car you've wrecked.

All of the justice in the world isn't fastened up in the courthouse.
☺Meaning: You don't need the law to tell you to do the right thing.

All the buzzards will come to the mule's funeral.
☺Meaning: All the relatives show up at a rich person's funeral.

Always drink pure water -many get drunk from breaking this rule.
☺"Drinking doesn't cause hangovers; stopping drinking causes hangovers." Lorenzo Music

An empty wagon makes a lot of noise.
☺Meaning: People who know nothing often talk the most.

An old sow knows enough about figures to count her pigs.
☺Meaning: Common sense comes in handy.

Anyone can fly - it's the landing that will kill you.
☺"The knack lies in learning how to throw yourself at the ground and miss." Douglas Adams.

Be like the old lady who fell out of the wagon.
☺Meaning: You weren't in the wagon, so stay out of it, i.e.– it's none of your business.

Beating a dead horse don't make it taste better.
☺China is the largest consumer of horse-meat, but many European countries indulge. There are no horse slaughterhouses in the US, but it's been legal since 2011.

Better gravy than no grease at all.
☺Note: To make gravy, you need grease. Mix equal part grease (Bacon drippings or flour work best) and flour into a paste, then add broth. Enjoy it on everything!

Better to keep your mouth shut and seem a fool than to open it and remove all doubt.
☺"Leadership to me means duty, honor, country. It means character, and it means listening from time to time."   George W. Bush

Between the bug and the Bee Martin, it ain't hard to tell which will get caught.
☺Note: Also known as "Kingbirds", "Bee Martins" are very aggressive. When defending their nests they will attack much larger predators like hawks, crows, and squirrels.

Birds of a feather flock together.
☺Note: This proverb has been in use since at least the mid-16th century.

Buzzards and chickens come home to roost.
☺Meaning: Your bad deeds will haunt you.

Church ain't over until the choir quits singing.
☺Note: "It ain't over till the fat lady sings." refers to Brunnhilde in Richard Wagner's Götterdämmerung,

Corn makes more at the mill than it does in the crib.
☺Meaning: A job 95% completed, is 100% incomplete.

Country fences need to be horse high, pig tight, and bull strong.
☺Note: Some farm animals, notably pigs and goats, are accomplished escape artists.

Crabgrass lines the path to the poorhouse.
☺Meaning: Appearances matter.

Crow and corn can't grow in the same field.
☺Meaning: One cannot serve two masters.

Do God's will - whatever the Hell it may be.
☺Meaning: Do the right thing, and let God take care of the rest.

Don't argue with idiots, they will drag you down to their level and beat you with experience.
☺Also: Don't wash a pig. They will enjoy it, they'll still be dirty and so will you.

Don't bite off more than you can chew.
☺Note: The record for eating Vienna Sausages is 8.31 lbs. in 10 Minutes by Sonya Thomas

Don't count your chickens until they hatch.
☺Note: The expected hatching rate is about 80% for chicks.

Don't ever wash a pig, you'll just get dirty, and the pig will enjoy it.
☺Meaning: Don't be tempted by someone baiting you to an argument or fight.

Don't fling away the empty wallet.
☺Meaning: Don't give up, fill up the wallet. Note: From Uncle Remus, His Songs and Sayings.

Don't get in a pissing contest with a polecat.
☺Note: If a skunk (polecat) sprays under your porch, fresh coffee put into a flat container and placed through the affected area. It will over power the smell but also absorb it.

Don't go off with your pistol half-cocked.
☺Meaning: Be prepared. Bring an umbrella (aka bumper shoot) just in case, and use a checklist.

Don't let the tail wag the dog.
☺Note: This saying was taken from the character Dundreary in the play "Our American Cousin" - the play Lincoln was watching on his assassination.

Don't let your mouth overload your tail.
☺Meaning: You don't have the collateral to back yourself up.

Don't start chopping until you've treed the coon.
☺Meaning: Don't jump to conclusions.

Don't sweat the petty things - pet the sweaty things.
☺Note: This phrase is known as a Dundrearyism (see "Our American Cousin") and is a proverb, colloquial phrase, saying or riddle humorously combined with another in such a way to render it nonsensical.

Don't take too big a start to jump a ditch.
☺Meaning: Stop stalling and just get on with it!

Don't trade off a coonskin before you catch the coon.
☺Meaning: Don't count your chickens.

Don't try to rake up the family secrets of every sausage you eat.
☺Rather than: Knowledge is knowing a tomato is a fruit. Wisdom is not putting it in a fruit salad.

Don't worry about the mule going blind just load the wagon.
☺Meaning: Let the boss worry about the mule, just do your job.

Don't corner something that you know is meaner than you.
☺Note: The "something" doesn't have to be meaner if it's cornered. Believe me.

Don't hang your wash on someone else's line.
☺Meaning: Be self-sufficient.

Don't judge folks by their relatives.
☺Meaning: You can find a peach in bushel of bad apples.

Don't name a pig you plan to eat.
☺Meaning: Pork chops make poor pets.

Don't rile the wagon master.

☺Meaning: Be nice to cab drivers.

Don't sell your mule to buy a plow.
☺Meaning: At least you can ride a mule: can't ride a plow.

Don't skinny dip with snapping turtles.
☺Meaning: You are liable to lose something you need.

Drinking wine today, picking grapes tomorrow.
☺Meaning: Fate is tricky, save for a rainy day.

Early bird gets the worm but the second mouse gets the cheese.
☺"Early to rise and early to bed makes a male healthy and wealthy and dead." James Thurber

Early don't last long.
☺Meaning: Let's get going.

Eat the frog.
☺Meaning: If you have a distasteful task, do it first thing.

Every day is just a role of the dice, and snake eyes is just a way of life.
☺Meaning: Fate and luck are fickle.

Every dog should have a few fleas.
☺Meaning: No one is perfect.

Everything that goes around at night ain't Santa Clause.
☺Meaning: Don't assume.

Fattened hogs ain't in luck.
☺Meaning: Fatten hogs are to be slaughtered.

Folks on the rich bottom land stop bragging when the river rises.
☺Meaning: Bottom land is the best for chops, however it is often flood prone.

Fools' names and fools' faces always appear in public places.
☺Note: Many families believe your name should appear only twice. Your wedding and obituary.

Good fences make good neighbors.
☺Meaning: Just that, but also get it in writing.

Ground sparrows will see the snowstorm way off.
☺Note: Falling air pressure caused by a coming storm causes discomfort in birds' ears, so they will fly low to alleviate it. Large numbers of birds roosting on power lines indicates swiftly falling air pressure.

Grubbing roots softens a straw bed.
☺Note: Grubbing means to clear land of roots and stumps by digging. You'll be tuckered afterwards.

Hair of the dog is good for the bite.
☺Meaning: If you just keep drinking, you'll never be hungover.

Hard liquor and a hammer ought to fix that.
☺ Go fetch a bigger hammer.

I been to two hog callings, a goat roast, and a World's Fair; and I still ain't never seen nothing like you.
☺Note: The oldest North American expo calling itself a World's Fair is the World's Fair of Tunbridge, Vermont, and assumed the name in 1867.

I'd take Heaven for the climate and Hell for the company.
☺Note: Another great quote form Mark Twain.

If a bullfrog had a glass ass, he'd only jump once.
☺Meaning: You shouldn't shoot your mouth off or press your luck.

If at first you don't succeed, use duct tape.

☺"If at first you don't succeed, find out if the loser gets anything."
William Lyon Phelps

If duct tape doesn't fix it - then you're not using enough duct tape."
☺"If at first you don't succeed, try, try again. Then quit. There's no
point in being a damn fool about it."   W. C. Fields

If I say a hen dips snuff, you can look under her wing for the can.
☺ Meaning: I know what I'm talking about – and you doubting me is
about to piss me off.

If you ain't the lead dog the scenery never changes.
☺Note: Another great quote from the late great Lewis Grizzard

If you buy a rainbow, don't pay cash for it.
☺Note: George C. Parker was the greatest con man in American
history and managed to sell landmarks like Madison Square
Gardens, the Statue of Liberty and the Brooklyn Bridge, often
several times in a day.

If you can't race it or take it to bed, you don't need it.
☺Also: Tell me what you want and I will tell you how to get along
without it.

If you cut your own firewood, it'll warm you twice.
☺Note: Splitting wood is a whole lotta' work.

If you don't have time to do it right when will you have time to do it
over?
☺Meaning: Do it right the first time

If you don't use your head, you might as well have two asses.
☺Also: Use your head for more than a hat-rack, son.

If you have to eat dirt, eat clean dirt.
☺Note: While most people would recoil at the thought of eating mud
or clay, some medical experts say it may be beneficial, especially for

pregnant women.

If you have to eat two frogs, eat the big one first.
☺Note: The long version and original version of Mark Twain's "eat the frog" saying.

If you lie down with dogs, you'll get up with fleas.
☺Meaning: Choose your friends wisely.

If you're bound to hang – you won't drown.
☺Note: In "Butch Cassidy" before they jump off a waterfall. Cassidy: "What's the matter with you?" Kid: "I can't swim." Cassidy: "Are you crazy? The fall will probably kill you."

It doesn't rain every time the pig squeals.
☺"Your assumptions are your windows on the world. Scrub them off every once in a while, or the light won't come in." Isaac Asimov

It doesn't take a very big person to carry a grudge.
☺"A grudge is like a cesspool; forgiveness like a flowing river."
Chris Northrup

It won't be long now, said the cat when they cut off its tail.
☺What did the monkey say when he caught his tail in the revolving door? A:"It won't be long now."

It'll all come out wash day.
☺Meaning: Everything happens for a reason.

It's easy to get off a bucking mule.
☺Meaning: Boasting about something easily achieved.

It's better to be pissed off then pissed on.
☺"Speak when you are angry - and you'll make the best speech you'll ever regret." Laurence J. Peter

It's hard to fly with the eagles when you run around with the turkeys.

☺Meaning: You've been invited to a "pity party".

Just because a chicken has wings doesn't mean it can fly.
☺"Beware of false knowledge; it is more dangerous than ignorance." George Bernard Shaw

Just do all you can do and let the rough end drag.
☺Meaning: If you have done your best then there is nothing more to be done.

Keep it up and I'll cancel your birth certificate.
☺If I tell you a duck can pull a truck, then hook the sucker up

Keep skunks and bankers at a distance.
☺Fact: Skunks often attack beehives because they like to eat honeybees.

Lazy folks' stomachs don't get tired.
☺Note: From Uncle Remus, His Songs and Sayings.

Let me tell you how the cow ate the cabbage.
☺Also: I can tell you a thing or two about a thing or two.

Let sleeping dogs lie.
☺Also: Let drowning cats swim.

Life is simpler when you plow around the stump.
☺Meaning: Don't be hardheaded.

Life is what you need, love is what you want.
☺"I have found that if you love life, life will love you back."
Arthur Rubinstein

Liquor talks mighty loud when it gets loose from the jug.
☺Fact: Your body releases dopamine when you drink. Dopamine blocks your brain's ability to make decisions.

Live and learn, die and know it all.
☺"You live and learn. At any rate, you live." Douglas Adams

Loading a wagon with hay isn't the quickest way to get religion.
☺Meaning: Save the Sabbath day for God.

Love many, trust few and always paddle your own canoe.
☺Meaning: Love, be wary, and be self-sufficient.

Make haste - there ain't no coming back.
☺"Do not squander time for that is the stuff life is made of." Ben Franklin

Make hay while the sun shines.
☺Note: Make moonshine while it's cloudy.

Many good cotton stalks get chopped by associating with weeds.
☺"A friend is one who walks in when others walk out." Walter Winchill

Meat fried before day won't last until night.
☺Note from the author: Not sure, but if I make too much fried anything I end up eating leftovers.

My dog sleeps in the garage, but it doesn't make him a truck.
☺Meaning: Rooting for the Patriots doesn't make you a cheater.

Never ask a barber if he thinks you need a haircut.
☺Note: Another favorite of Warren Buffett is: "An investor should act as though he had a lifetime decision card with just twenty punches on it."

Never bring a knife to a gun fight.
☺Rather than: Never bring a straw to a swimming pool.

Never climb an oak tree for pecans.
☺Rather than: Don't look for silver in a gold mine.

Never shake hands with a crayfish.
☺Note: Pinch their tails instead.

Never sign anything by neon.
☺Meaning: Do business with people you trust.

Never to go snipe hunting twice.
☺Rather than: Fool me once, shame on you. Fool me twice, shame on me.

Never trust a man too far who stays mad through Christmas week.
☺"I've had a few arguments with people, but I never carry a grudge. You know why? While you're carrying a grudge, they're out dancing." Buddy Hackett

Nightcrawlers aren't anxious for the fish to bite.
☺Meaning: Not everyone sees the world as you do.

No matter what you do to a skunk, it still stinks.
☺Note: If you or your pet has been sprayed, grab the hydrogen peroxide, baking soda, and dish-washing detergent.

Pigs don't know what a pen's for.
☺Note: Cannibals claim that humans taste similar to pork, and often refer to human flesh as "long pig" or "long pork."

Pigs get fat; hogs get slaughtered.
☺Meaning: Be satisfied with enough, too greedy will be your ruin.

Rails split before breakfast will season the dinner.
☺Fact: Amish farmers need to consume 4000 calories a day and maintain their weight.

Rheumatism and happiness both get bigger if you keep telling folks.
☺"Happiness can exist only in acceptance. George Orwell

Satan ain't scared of long sermons.
☺Meaning: Just because you sit in church doesn't mean you are a Christian.

Satan loads his cannons with big watermelons.
☺Meaning: Satan will tempt you fiercely. Rite of passage in the South is to do a midnight raid on a watermelon patch.

Save the pacing mare for Sunday.
☺Note: The pace is a lateral two-beat gait. In the pace, the two legs on the same side of the horse move forward together, unlike the trot, where the two legs diagonally opposite from each other move forward together.

Scared money don't win.
☺Meaning: Never bet more that you are willing to lose.

Setting hens don't hanker fresh eggs.
☺Meaning: There is an ulterior motive. Note: Setting (broody) hens are collecting eggs to hatch.

Skin your own buffalo.
☺Meaning: Be self-sufficient.

Soft ground tells a heap of tales.
☺Meaning: The evidence is clear to whatever you did.

Stump water won't cure the gripes.
☺Meaning: Drinking more isn't going to make you feel better.

Take the bit between your teeth.
☺Meaning: Give it 100% right now.

Teachers, bankers, and owls sleep with one eye open.
☺Fact: An owl has three eyelids: one for blinking, one for sleeping and one for keeping the eye clean.

Tell me what you need and I'll tell you how to get along without it.
☺Meaning: Ask me so I can say "no."

That possum's on the stump!
☺Meaning: That's good as it's going to get.

That rooster makes more racket than the hen that laid the egg.
☺"If a June night could talk, it would probably boast it invented romance." Bernard Williams

The Black Gum laughs at the Red Oak when the woodcutter comes around.
☺Note: The wood of the Black Gum is heavy, hard, cross-grained, and difficult to split.

The bullfrog never makes a mistake when he starts singing.
☺Meaning: The best time to start is always now.

The cotton patch doesn't care which way you vote.
☺Meaning: Whoever is in the White House won't be helping you feed your family.

The devil has no particular objection to Christmas.
☺Meaning: Celebrating Easter and Christmas doesn't make you a Christian.

The dinner bell's always in tune.
☺Rather than: Call me anything but "Late for dinner."

The hawk would like to get a job in the chicken yard keeping away the minks.
☺Meaning: It might not be a good idea to hire a thief to catch a thief.

The jay-bird doesn't rob his own nest.
☺Fact: If an owl roosts near the nest during the daytime the blue jay mobs it until it takes a new roost.

The man that always takes the shortest road to a dollar generally takes the longest road away from it.
☺Meaning: Avoid get rich quick schemes.

The mosquito says grace too loud for his own good before getting ready.
☺Meaning: Don't boast.

The mule doesn't pull so well with a mortgage on his back.
☺Meaning: Don't borrow money.

The mule that chews up his own collar is fixing for a sore shoulder.
☺Meaning: Don't shoot yourself in the foot.

The north wind knows all the cracks in the house.
☺Meaning: The faults in your plan will be made apparent.

The otter would have more peace if his clothes weren't so fine.
☺Meaning: Don't show off.

The partridge that makes a nest in a wheat field won't be pestered by her chicks.
☺Meaning: Take time to keep the brood busy so you can have more time for yourself.

The quickest way to double your money is to fold it over and put it back in your pocket.
☺Note: Warren Buffett's Advice: Forget Get-Rich-Quick. Get Rich Slowly.

The rabbit is too honest to steal grapes, and the fox is too honest to steal cabbage.
☺Meaning: Most people can be trusted with things they do not want.

The rabbit thinks experience costs too much if you get it from a trap.
☺Also: Live and learn. Die and know it all.

The road to Hell is paved with good intentions.
☺Note: The saying is thought to have originated with Saint Bernard of Clairvaux, c. 1150.

The terrapin walks fast enough to go visiting.
☺Rather than: You may not get what you want, but you have what you need.

The woodpile doesn't grow much on frosty nights.
☺Meaning: Prepare for the tough times.

There's more than one way to break a dog from sucking eggs.
☺Note: Apparently dogs have a taste for eggs, once they discover them, it's difficult to keep them from eating eggs.

There's no need for pockets on a dead man's coat.
☺Meaning: You can't take it with you.

This ain't my first rodeo.
☺Rather than: I've been down this path before.

Those who know too much sleep under the ash-hopper.
☺Note: From Uncle Remus, His Songs and Sayings.

Throw it up to the wind and let the dust settle it.
☺Meaning: You have done what you can, all you can do it wait and see.

To know how country folks are doing, look at their barns, not their houses.
☺Meaning: Farmers put their money into things that can return an investment.

Tomorrow may be the carriage-driver's day for plowing.
☺Meaning: Have a plan "B".

Tomorrow's ash-cake is better than last Sunday's pudding.

☺Note: An "ash cake" of corn meal baked in hot ashes. Better than old pudding. But you gotta work for it.

Trying to understand some folks is like guessing at the direction of a rat hole underground.
☺Note: Rat holes usually have three exits.

Turnip tops don't tell you the size of the turnips.
☺Rather than: Don't judge a book by its cover.

Two can live as cheap as one if one don't eat.
☺Note: Another great Quote from Will Rogers: "There are three kinds of men. The one that learns by reading. The few who learn by observation. The rest of them have to pee on the electric fence for themselves."

Water meets its own level.
☺Meaning: Quality people of integrity find other quality people of integrity.

What you can learn by boxing with a left-hander costs more than it's worth.
☺A study suggests that because humans are highly cooperative, this has resulted in a right-handed majority.

What you don't have in your head, you have to have in your feet.
☺Meaning: You can choose your own path.

When it takes half a sandwich to catch a catfish, let him alone.
☺Meaning: It's more efficient to eat the sandwich.

When life gives you scraps, make a quilt.
☺ "If life gives you lemons, find someone who life is giving them vodka." Ron White.

When you find yourself in a hole - quit digging.
☺"Insanity: doing the same thing over and over again and expecting

different results." Albert Einstein

When you got nothing to say, you say it.
☺Meaning: Say what you were going to say at your own risk.

When you wallow with pigs, expect to get dirty.
☺Meaning: You're known by the company you keep.

Whip a horse with oats.
☺Rather than: You catch more bees with honey than vinegar.

Words that soak best into ears are whispered.
☺Meaning: Use subterfuge to get your point across.

You can hide the fire, but what will you do with the smoke?
☺Note: The "Dakota Fire Hole" is a technique where the flames are below ground, and so the fire burns hotter, producing less smoke.

You can pick your friends and you can pick your nose - but you can't wipe your friends on your saddle.
☺This is a "Dundreary-ism" or a reverse play on words

You can't get blood from a turnip.
☺Note: Another turn-about might be" You can't get a rock by squeezing a turnip."

You can't judge the depth of a well by the handle of the pump.
☺ All that glitters isn't gold.

You can't make a silk purse out of a sow's ear.
☺"A girl on spring break is there to be met. A pig ear sammwich is there to be et. So don't be shy about one or the other, if that gal turns you down, just go ask another. A pig ear sammwich is a real salty treat. The gal on spring break is just waitin' to meet . So hose down real good and brush that one tooth. Take her to supper and ask for a booth. Them gals on spring break just comes 'round once a year. If you blow this one chance, you still got that ear."... Don Drane

You can't tell much about a chicken pie until you get through the crust.
☺Meaning: Don't be quick to judge.

You can't get lard unless you boil the hog.
☺Advice to someone who is hesitant to do a difficult task.

You can't have chicken salad without the chicken shit.
☺Meaning: You've got to take the good with the bad.

You can't unsay a cruel word.
☺Rather than: Think before you speak.

You don't have a lick of sense!
☺Also: Bless your heart, you are an idiot.

You got to be 10% smarter than the equipment you're running.
☺Note: The 10% model also refers to food chains. In food chains, the predator only gains about ten percent of the prey's energy. This pyramid effect leads to lower populations of top predators.

You might as well die with the chills as with the fever.
☺Meaning: If you going to meet the same ends, it won't matter how you get there.

You will go to Hell for lying just as well stealing.
☺When you tell a lie, you steal someone's right to the truth.

You'll lose your grip if you put too much spit on your hands.
☺Meaning: Get on with it.

Scrawny: They look poorly.

In 2010, the Centers for Disease Control and Prevention categorized over 2/3rds of Americans as overweight. The National Institutes of Health came out with their study that found that all adults categorized as overweight and most of those categorized as obese have a lower mortality risk than so-called normal-weight individuals. So that about a third of Americans would categorized as overweight would be re-categorized as normal weight instead.

In my study, the number of Southern Sayings for fat and thin are both around a dozen. This infers than there were as many thin people as fat. Here is how you comment on the thin ones.

A strong fart in a whirlwind would blow him away.
☺Rather than: He tripped, hit the curb and shattered.

He could fall through his ass and hang himself.
☺Rather than: He uses dental floss for toilet paper.

He looks wormy.
☺Rather than: He had to stand in the same place twice to cast a shadow.

He sure is poor.
☺Rather than: They couldn't find him in this joke.

He swapped legs with a jaybird and got cheated out of a butt.
☺Rather than: Wears waders in the shower to keep from slipping down the drain.

He'd have to stand up twice to cast a shadow.
☺Rather than: His laptop seats 12 of him.

He's only got one stripe on his pajamas.
☺Rather than: He uses Chapstick as a body moisturizer.

His pants had only one back pocket.
☺Rather than: His pants have one belt loop.

If she stood sideways and stuck out her tongue she'd look like a zipper.
☺Rather than: When she wears yellow people mistake her for a No. 2 pencil.

She could tread water in a test-tube.
☺Rather than: I've seen better legs on chickens.

She's a carpenter's dream: flat as a board and ain't never been nailed.
☺Rather than: If she turned sideways and stuck out her tongue, she would look like a zipper.

Shiftless: As useful as tits on a tricycle.

Southerners admire enterprise, and will set their scrutiny on anyone who is slacking. When young William Faulkner came home after serving in the Royal Flying Corps, he affected British mannerisms and he was often seen in his airman uniform loafing around town. His pose earned him the nickname "Count No 'Count."

Faulkner would soon redeem himself to Southerners of course, but not simply because of to his fame as a writer. He was among several Nobel Prize laureates invited by President Kennedy to a White House dinner. At the time the novelist was teaching at the University of Virginia. He declined, saying: "Why that's a hundred miles away. That's a long way to go just to eat."

Word to the wise: Be careful to whom you call shiftless.

About as useful as buttons on a dishrag.
☺Rather than: As useful as a hand knitted condom

Ain't worth the salt in her bread.
☺Rather than: As useful as a fart in a hurricane

Ain't worth the wagon he rode in on.
☺Rather than: As useful as a third armpit

Ain't nothin' but a hound dog.
☺Rather than: Useful as an ashtray on a tricycle.

All hat and no cow.
☺Note: Some of the British versions are worth repeating: all mouth and no trousers, fur coat and no knickers, no bell on your bike, and your knickers at half-mast.

As much good as windshield wipers on a ducks butt.
☺Note: Rainy weather is usually good hunting, "blue sky" often not.

Couldn't carry a tune in a bushel basket.
☺Rather than: As useful as a truckload of Chihuahuas

Couldn't herd ducks to water in front of a pond.
☺Note: In China, the Bible's translation of "The Good Shepherd" is: "Good Duck Man."

Couldn't hit a bull in the ass with a bass fiddle.
☺Fact: The double bass is the only bowed string instrument that is tuned in fourths, rather than fifths.

Couldn't pour piss out of a boot with the instructions printed on the heel.
☺Note: The visual is the key to this saying. It would be impossible not to pour it out.

Couldn't teach a settin' hen to cluck.
☺Note: Chickens are actually playful if given space. They will run, jump, spa and even sunbathe.

Dumber than a barrel of spit and half as useful.
☺Note: Spittoons or cuspidors were once a fixture in hotel lobbies, railroad stations, and saloons.

Handy as a cow on crutches.
☺Note: Cows may be saved, but a bull with a fractured leg is game over because of breeding.

He couldn't find his own ass with both hands stuck in his back pockets.
☺"Never ascribe to malice that which can adequately be explained by incompetence." Napoleon Bonaparte

He couldn't hit the broad side of a barn if he was inside it.
☺"If at first you don't succeed, you may be at your level of incompetence already." Dr. Laurence J. Peter

He couldn't organize a pissing contest in a brewery.
☺Fact: There are written recipes for beer that date to 5,000 BC.

He couldn't carry a tune in a bucket.
☺Rather than: As useful as dinosaur repellent

He couldn't hit his own ass with directions and a map.
☺"Super-competence is more objectionable than incompetence."
...Peter's Observation.

He couldn't hit the water if he fell out the boat.
☺"Employees in a hierarchy do not really object to incompetence in their colleagues." Peter's Paradox

He's about as useful as a steering wheel on a mule.
☺Rather than: He could throw himself on the ground and miss.

He's about as useless as a bent dog pecker.
☺Fact: A dog penis has a bone that can be fractured. Symptoms of a canine penis fracture includes difficulty urinating, frequent urinary tract infections, discharge, excessive licking and a dog that is straining to pee.

He's no 'count.
☺Coming home to Oxford, MS in 1918 after serving in the Royal Flying Corps, William Faulkner was given the nickname: "Count No 'Count."

He's a legend in his own mind.
☺"I won't be a rock star. I will be a legend." Freddie Mercury

He's about as handy as a back pocket on a shirt.
☺Note: The first pockets were actually small pouches that hung from the belt where one could carry valuables and coins.

He's about as useful as a pogo stick in quicksand.

☺Note: The sport of Extreme Pogo, or Xpogo, was introduced around 1999 using poles that can reach 10 feet in length.

He's as useful as a tit on a boar hog.
☺He's useful as tits on a Light-bulb, bullfrog or bicycle.

I need him like a tomcat needs a trousseau.
☺Rather than: As useful as a concrete life-vest

If he had a third hand he'd need an extra pocket to stick it in.
☺"Any man who reads too much and uses his own brain too little falls into lazy habits of thinking."   Albert Einstein

Like a milk pail under a bull.
☺Fact: A bull may service 50 to 60 cows during a breeding season.
Note: It's good to be the king.

Never set a river on fire.
☺Note: The Cuyahoga River in Cleveland, polluted from decades of industrial waste, caught fire in 1969 near the Republic Steel mill and caused damage to two railroad bridges.

That boy has a lot of quit in him.
☺"My father was a quitter, my grandfather was a quitter, I was raised to give up. It's one of the few things I do well."   Jason Alexander

Too mean for Jesus and too dumb for the Devil.
☺Note: Possible answer to the question: "What do Washington and Media have in common?"

Useful as a bull at a square dance.
☺"A lot of critics are lazy. They don't want to look closely and analyze something for what it is. They take a quick first impression and then rush to compare it to something they've seen before."
William Dafoe

Useful as a screen door on a submarine.
☺Note: "Bug Juice" is a Kool-Aid-like beverage in dispensers on the mess-decks.

Useful as a trap door on a canoe.
☺Note: The word 'canoe' originated from the word "kenu" meaning "dugout." These seagoing boats were used by the Caribe Indians of the Caribbean.

Useful as an ashtray on a motorcycle.
☺Rather than: Useful as a convent camisole.

Useless as hen-shit on a pump handle.
☺Rather than: Useless as a pump handle on a mule.

Useless as teats on a light-bulb.
☺Rather than: As useful as forward gears on an Iraqi tank

Worthless as a sidesaddle on a sow.
☺Note: It's best to ride a pig back on the haunches.

Skinflints: He knows every dollar by first name.

Cheapskates don't revel in consumerism. Like previous generations of Americans, for whom thrift and frugality were considered virtues, they believe in using things up, wearing things out, and making things last. In the US, 80 percent of people experience buyer's remorse on discretionary items.

We like to make fun, but there is a lesson here. Certainly the US Government could learn a thing or two. Hopefully you can use these terms to describe the folks spending our tax dollars.

Close chewer and tight spitter.
☺Rather than: So cheap, he brings popcorn to the movies and asks them to pop it.

Fast with his hat and slow with his money.
☺Rather than: He's not cheap, but he is on special this week.

He knows every dollar by first name.
☺Rather than: He still has the first dollar he ever borrowed

He squeezes a quarter so tight the eagle screams.
☺Fact: The edges on coins were developed to prevent thieves from shaving gold & silver off of the coins

He wouldn't pay a nickel to see a piss ant pull a freight train.
☺Fact: Railroad track reached its peak in 1916 in the United States.

He'd squeeze a nickel until the buffalo farts.
☺"His money is twice tainted: taint yours and taint mine."   Mark Twain

He's tighter than a bull's ass at fly time.
☺Note: To keep flies away for the barn, put a penny in a plastic bag

of water over the stall.

His ass squeaks when he walks.
☺Note: Around 7% of ceramic hips squeak.

If he walks over a penny, his butt quivers.
☺"If all the rich people in the world divided up their money among themselves, there wouldn't be enough to go around." Christina Stead

She wouldn't give a nickel to see Jesus riding a bicycle.
☺Rather than: So cheap he borrowed a suit to be buried in.

Tighter than a flea's ass over a rain barrel.
☺Rather than: He breathes through his nose to keep from wearing out his teeth.

Tighter than a tick.
☺"I once gave Gracie a coupon for a year's subscription to a magazine as a gift – and all she had to do was fill it out and send it in with a check." George Burns

Tighter than bark on a tree.
☺"He's the only man I ever knew who had rubber pockets so he could steal soup." Wilson Mizner

Tighter than Dick's hat-band.
☺Rather than: He's a wolf in "cheap" clothing.

When he smiles his eyes curl up.
☺Rather than: He makes pancakes so thin they've got just one side to them.

When he walks over a penny his butt quivers.
☺"I'm half Scottish and half Jewish, so don't ask me for money." David Duchovny

Speed – Faster: than a frog shot out of a barn.

Sprinter Michael Johnson is considered one of the greatest sprinters in the history of track and field. He won four Olympic gold medals and eight World Championship gold medals. Johnson holds or held, records in the 400 m. 200 m, and 300 m. His record 200 m time of 19.32 at the 1996 Summer Olympics stood for over 12 years. He is tied with Carl Lewis and Usain Bolt for the most gold medals won by a runner. He broke 44 seconds for the 400 metres twenty-two times, more than twice as many times as any other athlete.

Michael Johnson is from Dallas, now living in California. If you see him or his children, you might be tempted to use these phrases.

Fast as all get out.
☺"Light thinks it travels faster than anything but it is wrong. No matter how fast light travels, it finds the darkness has always got there first, and is waiting for it." Terry Pratchett

Fast as greased lightning.
☺"I drive way too fast to worry about cholesterol." Steven Wright

Faster than a bee stung stallion.
☺Note: The highest race speed for a horse is recorded at 43.97 miles per hour by Winning Brew in 2008.

Faster than a bell clapper in a goose's ass.
☺Note: The waddle of a goose is referred to as a "bell-clapper gait.

Faster than a cat can lick its ass.
☺Note: A cat's scat is one of the fastest ways to help determine what might be wrong with an ailing cat.

Faster than a frog shot through a barn.
☺Rather than: Faster than a dog shot through a barn.

Faster than a hot knife through butter.
☺Note: Salted butter will keep for twice as long as un-salted.

Faster than a monkey on moonshine.
☺Note: Monkeys, not surprisingly, fall into the same patterns as humans: abstinence, social drinking, heavy drinking, and abusive drinking.

Faster than a one-legged man in a butt-kicking competition.
☺Note: Matt Betzold, the fighter who lost half of his left leg at the age of 6, is a professional MMA fighter.

Faster than a striped assed ape.
☺Rather than: Faster than a raped ape.

Faster than green grass through a goose.
☺Note: The best way to get rid of geese is to invite them to Thanksgiving.

He can blow out the lamp and jump into bed before the room gets dark.
☺"I'm so fast that last night I turned off the light switch in my hotel room and was in bed before the room was dark." Muhammad Ali

He can turn off the switch and jump in bed before it gets dark.
☺Rather than: Faster than a dog shot through a barn.

He ran like a scalded haint.
☺Note: Blue porches in the South are often seen because it was thought to fool wasps into thinking the ceiling was the sky and also to scare away ghosts by fooling them into thinking it was daylight.

He ran like his feet were on fire and his butt was catching.
☺Note: Usain Bolt, who has clocked nearly 28 mph; however, science has concluded that the upper limit is 40 mph for humans.

He went through that like Sherman went through Georgia.

☺Note: Despite his reputation for "hard" warfare, Sherman granted general amnesty to the rebels upon swearing an oath of allegiance.

I am off like a dirty shirt!
☺Note: Wicking fabric works by pulling moisture to the exterior of the shirt where it can evaporate more easily.

It happened faster than a knife fight in a phone booth.
☺Note: The phone booth was invented by William Gray in 1889. It was installed in a Connecticut bank, and oddly- callers paid after the call was finished.

Like a dose of salts through a widow woman.
☺Note: Stars such as Gwyneth Paltrow and Victoria Beckham bathe in Epsom salts for flat stomach.

Like a duck on a June bug.
☺"Time flies like an arrow. Fruit flies like a banana." Grouch Marx

Quick as a politician's promise.
☺Note: The only substitute for good manners is fast reflexes.

Ran like a turpentine-ed cat.
☺Note: Turpentine is distilled pine resin used mainly as a solvent. Running like the house is on fire.
☺Word to the wise: Don't deep fry a frozen turkey in the garage.

Took off like Moody's goose.
☺Note: Moody was a Ford engineer for the model A, which had a quail hood ornament. As the car sold well, it "took off." I suppose "goose" is funnier than "quail."

Slower than a drunk snail crawling on molasses up an ice hill in January.
☺Note: One of the best ways to catch these garden pests is with a bowl of beer.

Speed – Slower: than a herd of turtles racing in peanut butter.

It's a well-worn cliché that the pace is slower in the South. Honestly, I used to dread arriving in the Memphis airport to visit my folks. After New York, everything was so bland: no honking horns, sweaty crowds or fermenting garbage. How to people live like this!!!

Life is slower here. Why would you want to rush life? These Southernisms for slow may help you cope.

He runs just like a candle.
☺Fact: Candle manufacturers' surveys show that 96% of all candles purchased are bought by women.

He was moving so slow, dead flies wouldn't fall off of him.
☺ Slower than a seven year itch.

He's slower than a two legged coon dog on a Monday morning.
☺Fact: According to the ASPCA, a paw massage will relax your dog and promote better circulation. They recommend rubbing between the pads on the bottom of the paw, and then rubbing between each toe.

Last hog to the trough.
☺Fact: Most farmers use corn or soybean meal as the main ingredient in a pig diet.

Like a cat eating a grindstone.
☺Meaning: Do whatever you're doing slowly and gently.

She has two speeds. Slow and stop.
☺Note: By strength-training just a couple of times a week, for example, you'll reverse 50% of the seemingly inevitable metabolism slow-down that comes with age.

Slower than a herd of turtles stampeding through peanut butter.
☺Fact: The average American child will eat 1,500 peanut butter and jelly sandwiches before graduating high school.

Slower than a Sunday afternoon.
☺Fact: Any regular Sunday social ritual—church for some, yoga or softball for others—can lift spirits.

Slower than cream rising on last year's buttermilk.
☺Fact: Originally, buttermilk was the liquid left behind after churning butter out of cream.

Slower than molasses running uphill in January.
☺Fact: On January 15, 1919, Boston suffered one of history's strangest disasters: a devastating flood of 2.3 gallons of molasses. The poorly constructed holding tank broke, sending a flood that ripped buildings from their foundations.

Slower than pond water.
☺Note: During the winter, it is important to keep a small portion of the pond surface from freezing for oxygenation.

Slower than turtles racing in molasses.
☺Fact: A box turtle can run up to 4 miles per hour – for very short distances.

We're off like a herd of turtles.
☺Note: A group of turtles is called a "bale."

Surprised: Knock me over with a feather duster.

Note: This is an actual letter to the Principal of the Safety Harbor Middle School:

Dear Safety Harbor Middle School:

God blesses you for the beautiful radio I won at your recent senior citizens luncheon. I am 84 years old and live at the Safety Harbor Assisted Home for the Aged. All of my family has passed away. I am all alone now and it's nice to know that someone is thinking of me.

God bless you for your kindness to an old forgotten lady. My roommate is 95 and always had her own radio, but before I received one, she would never let me listen to hers, even when she was napping.

The other day her radio fell off the night stand and broke into a lot of pieces. It was awful and she was in tears. She asked if she could listen to mine, and I said, "Fuck you."

Life is good.

Sincerely,

Edna

Edna's roommate got her comeuppance, here's how to express her surprise.

Caught with your pants down.
☺"If you expect nothing, you're apt to be surprised. You'll get it."
Malcolm Forbes

I was as surprised as if a sheep had bit me.
☺Note: Sheep have very good memories, they can remember at least 50 individual sheep and humans for years. If you are "ugly" to a sheep, don't be surprised if it takes a nip at you.

If it'd been a snake it would have bit you.
☺"The husband who decides to surprise his wife is often very much surprised himself." Voltaire

Knock me over with a feather!
☺Behind every successful man is a proud wife and a surprised mother-in-law.

Like finding a diamond in a billy goat's butt.
☺"Expect the best, plan for the worst, and prepare to be surprised." Denis Waitley

Like finding a feather on a frog.
☺Note: Frogs will eat birds, and anything else that they can swallow.

Makes a bulldog want to hug a ham.
☺Note: The most expensive hams are from Spain. The acorn-rich diet transforms the fat of the jamón ibérico de bellota. More than half the ham's fat content is monounsaturated so that it virtually melts at room temperature.

So surprised you could have knocked his eyes off with a stick.
☺Note: When I was born I was so surprised I didn't talk for a year and a half." Gracie Allen

Stick a paper umbrella up my butt and call me a hurricane.
☺"I was elated, ecstatic and extremely surprised that we were successful." Neil Armstrong

That takes the cake.
☺Also: That takes the gravy.

Well don't that beat a goose gobbling!
☺"One bad thing about Lassie, she was always warning you about something; let me be surprised for a change." Jack Handey

Well I'll be a sock-eyed mule!

☺I was as surprised as if a sheep had bit me.

Well, ain't that the cat's pajamas!
☺Note: Coined in the jazz era of the 1920's.

Well, shut my mouth!
☺"You'd be surprised how much fun you can have sober. When you get the hang of it." James Pinckney Miller

Well, slap my head and call me silly!
☺Also: Well doggies. Notes: Thank you Uncle Jed.

Whatever cranks your tractor!
☺Rather than: Whatever floats your Barcalounger.

You scared the living day lights out of me.
☺Fact: When startled, the brain releases glutamate and a second signal to the hypothalamus which triggers our autonomic nervous system — the system responsible for the superman mode.

Threats: You're going to Hell on a scholarship.

Imagine for a moment you're an alumnus of the Big Ten. You're at a spontaneously thrown party next door. The topic is football. After you give a 30 minute discourse on how over rated the SEC is, you've noticed that the room has suddenly cleared out, but cannot fathom why. Here are the sayings you probably missed while talking.

<u>Boy, don't let me start the head lights on the hearse.</u>
☺Meaning: I brought you into this world, I can take you out!

<u>Cain't never could.</u>
☺Meaning: You better start running.

<u>Don't start none....there won't be none!"</u>
☺Meaning: Zip it up before it's too late

<u>Don't let your mouth write a check your butt can't cash.</u>
☺None but a coward dares to boast that he has never known fear."
Ferdinand Foch

<u>Don't make me open up a can of whup ass!</u>
☺Fact: A can of "Whoop Ass" can be bought online for about $3.25.

<u>Give me the bacon without the sizzle.</u>
☺Meaning: Just the facts please.

<u>Go cork your pistol.</u>
☺Meaning: Please stop talking.

<u>Go peddle your own produce.</u>
☺Meaning: I don't believe your BS.

<u>Go pound salt up your ass with a wire brush.</u>
☺Meaning: Go screw yourself.

Good night nurse!
☺Meaning: That's it. I've had enough.

He didn't know whose weeds he was pissing in.
☺Meaning: They were ill advised.

I didn't just fall off the turnip truck yesterday.
☺ I didn't just fall off the pumpkin wagon.

I don't give a hoot 'n holler.
☺Note: Hoot and holler is also a communications system where there is a permanent open circuit between parties.

I wouldn't give you air if you were in a jug.
☺ I wouldn't walk across the street to piss on you if you were on fire.

I'll be all over you like stink on a skunk.
☺ I'll be on you like flies on shit.

I'll beat you like a rented mule.
☺Note: I wouldn't, mules can be vindictive. But, like a rental car, you're not as careful as you might be.

I'll get all over you like white on rice.
☺ Like stink on shit.

I'll jerk a knot in your tail!
☺Note: "Limber tail" is a condition where the dog's tail tendons have been strained due to overexertion, or cold water.

I'll knock you so hard you'll see tomorrow today.
☺Note: Austria is about 10 hours ahead, which means if you deck somebody at happy hour it is tomorrow today.

I'll put a knot on your head a calf could suck.
☺Note: If you calf doesn't suckle, put some white chocolate in its mouth with your fingers.

I'll slap some stuff on your head Ajax won't take off.
☺Note: Since 1947, the ingredients of Ajax include quartz as a scouring agent.

I'll slap you so hard you'll starve to death before you stop falling.
☺Fact: Vesna Vulović, a Serbian flight attendant, holds the record of surviving an estimated 33,000 ft. fall.

I'll stomp a mud hole in your butt and walk it dry.
☺Meaning: I am going to kick your arse.

I'm fixin' to shut out the lights.
☺Note: "Fixin'" means "going to do something."

I'm gonna cloud up and make it rain.
☺You can create your own rain cloud in a coke bottle. Google for the "how to."

I'm gonna cut your tail!
☺Note: Lizards will often lose their tails when a predator grasps it. To do this, the lizard contracts segmented muscles to disrupt the adhesive forces that keep the segments together...

I'm gonna jerk you through a knot.
☺Note: A stopper knot is tied at the end of a rope to prevent the end from slipping back through.

I'm gonna slap you so hard when you quit rolling' your clothes will be outta style.
☺Fact: Mohan Das, known as the "rolling saint" is an Indian holy man promoting peace by traveling 19,000 miles by rolling on the ground. He averages seven miles a day often smoking a cigarette while in transit.

I got a bone to pick with you.
☺Rather than: Take my advice — I'm not using it.

I'll hit you so hard your whole family will hurt!
☺Fact: A professional boxer can hit with up to 1200lbs of force per square inch.

I'll kill you and tell God you died.
☺"Did you think I'd forgotten you? Perhaps you hoped I had."
Frank Underwood

I'll knock a knot on your head so tall you'll have to climb a ladder to comb your hair.
☺Fact: Known as the Immovable Ladder, this latter has remained in a Jerusalem temple in the same spot since 1757.

I'll skin you like a Georgia catfish.
☺Also: I'll skin you like a Kentucky Carp.

I'll smack you so hard your kids will come out behaving.
☺Note: Approximately 60% of adults still approve of physical punishment, despite compelling evidence that it does not work, it makes things worse.

I'm gonna put a knot in your head the Boy Scouts can't get out.
☺Note: According to the World Organization of the Scouting Movement, all but six countries make Scouting available to their youthful citizenry.

It ain't bragging' if you can back it up.
☺"If you done it, it ain't bragging." Walt Whitman

It takes money to ride the train and drink liquor.
☺Meaning: Be quiet, I don't have enough money to buy what you are selling.

Let 'er rip - tater chip.
☺Note: The "let'er rip" phrase was first printed in a book titled "Out West", c. 1910.

<u>May God bless your soul, but I have your hide.</u>
☺"May God have mercy on General Lee, for I will have none."...US General Joe Hooker before his defeat at Chancellorsville.

<u>Me and you are gonna go to fist city.</u>
☺Note: "Fist City" was written by Loretta Lynn in 1968 and was inspired by her husband's dalliances with other women who pursued him while she was busy touring. It was a threat to those other women.

<u>My momma didn't drop me off the tater wagon.</u>
☺Note: Russet skinned potatoes do not grow well in the South. Pick white- or red-skinned types as well as those with yellow, pink or purplish flesh.

<u>My cow died last night, so I don't need your bull.</u>
☺Rather than: Lie to your friends, don't lie to me.

<u>Not worth the powder and shot it'd take to blow you to church.</u>
☺Meaning: Whatever you showed me really stinks.

<u>Ohhh Hell no!</u>
☺Note. Primarily heard from a female, if this phrase is directed at you, start running - whatever gender you are.

<u>Take your head out of your ass.</u>
☺Note: To get by censors, try using the English term "arse" instead of "ass" or "butt."

<u>That truck couldn't pull a fat baby off a tricycle.</u>
☺Note: The late model F150 has a towing capacity of 12,200lbs. It would tow about 400 strollers.

<u>They better not darken my doorway!</u>
☺Note: Benjamin Franklin used the phrase in The Busybody (1729): "I am afraid she would resent it so as never to darken my doors again."

The last time I saw a mouth that big it had a hook in it.
☺"I took her to the top of the Empire State building and planes started to attack her."   Rodney Dangerfield

The only thing that separates you from white trash is your rich husband.
☺"It's a new low for actresses when you have to wonder what's between her ears instead of her legs."   Katharine Hepburn

Whatever blows your dress up.
☺ Whatever bloats your goat.

When it doubt, knock him out!
☺Fact: Thai prisoners are released early if they take part in special kick-boxing matches against foreigners.

Who's plucking this chicken, you or me?
☺Meaning: Don't interrupt, I'm telling this story.

You are barking up the wrong tree.
☺Note: The earliest known printed citation is in James Kirke Paulding's Westward Ho!, 1832.

You ain't through climbing fool's hill yet.
☺"He is so stupid you can't trust him with an idea."   John Steinbeck

You ain't nothing but a piss ant in the big ant hill of life.
☺Note: U.S. President Lyndon B. Johnson referred to Vietnam as "a piddling piss-ant little country"

You are full of gas with nowhere to go.
☺ Rather than: Why don't you let that hole under your nose heal up?

You can put a coat and tie on a turd, but it's still gonna be a turd.
☺Rather than: After meeting you, I've decided I am in favor of abortion.

You can't make chicken salad out of chicken shit.
☺Rather than: I heard you changed your mind. What did you do with the diaper?

You could start an argument in an empty house.
☺Rather than: Don't believe everything you think.

You're like a bad penny.
☺Rather than: If things get any worse, I'll have to ask you to stop helping me.

You're as smart as you are good looking - and that ain't saying much.
☺Rather than: She's got a body that won't quit and a brain that won't start.

You don't know doodley squat.
☺Note: "Bo" Jackson and Bo Diddley put the saying in the mainstream with, "Bo, you don't know Diddley!"

You don't know dip shit from apple butter!
☺Note: Apple butter made by slow cooking crushed apples with cider until it caramelizes.

You lie like a cheap rug.
☺Rather than: You lie like a tombstone.

You lie like a dirty cur dog.
☺Note: Cur dogs are specialized, multipurpose working/hunting dogs from the southern USA. Each Cur breed or type is unique. Curs are usually not recognized as show dogs, but developed solely for their hunting ability.

You mess with the bull, you get the horns.
☺Note: In rodeo, animals account for half of the overall score. While riders are judged on their technique, horses and bulls are scored on the strength of the jumps and speed of their turns.

<u>You're going to Hell on a scholarship.</u>
☺Note from the author: I hope Hell is cheaper than college. Or did I just answer the question?

<u>You're gonna catch nine shades of Hell.</u>
☺Note: In Dante's Divine Comedy, the shades, (i.e. the souls of the damned), stand at the entrance to Hell, pointing to the inscription, Abandon hope, all ye who enter here."

<u>You're talking like a man with a paper butt.</u>
☺Meaning: A person with a paper ass lacks substance.

<u>Your promise is like snow in July.</u>
☺"Figures won't lie, but liars can figure."   Fletcher Knebel

Time: You can't hurry up good times by waiting for them.

My grandfather used to say: Funny how time passes. I've had two bypasses, a hip replacement, two new knees, survived prostate cancer and diabetes. I'm half blind, can't hear anything without a hearing aid that I don't wear. My medications that make me dizzy, winded, and subject to blackouts. I have dementia and circulation so bad sometimes I can hardly feel my hands and feet. I'm not sure if I'm 88 or 90. But, thank God, I still have my driver's license!

Ain't been home since Josie was a calf.
☺"Josie Basset was known as the Queen of the Rustlers, and was a pioneer women with a life worth exploring.

As long as Pat stayed in the army.
☺Meaning: Not long.

Back when men were men and sheep were nervous.
☺Rather than: Back when men were men.

By and by.
☺Note: The meaning of the term has changed from referring to a "near" time to a term for the hereafter.

Did it in a fever.
☺Meaning: Did it in a rush.

Don't spoil Saturday night by counting the time to Monday morning.
☺"Stephen and Time are now both even. Stephen beat Time and now Time's beat Stephen." A gravestone epitaph

From now until Gabriel blows his horn.
☺Meaning: From now until judgment day.

I got up at the butt-crack of dawn.
☺ Note: "Arse crack" if you're being censored.

I will be along directly.
☺Meaning: Whenever I am good and ready.

It's time to fish or cut bait.
☺Note: The original expression was "fish or cut bait or go ashore,"

Pulled too green.
☺Meaning: Something begun before the person is ready.

Root hog or die.
☺Note: Idiom from the early colonial practice of turning pigs loose in the woods to fend for themselves and is an expression for self-reliance.

Slap some bacon on biscuit.
☺Meaning: Let's move out, we're wasting time...

That won't last two foggy mornings.
☺Meaning: A comment on a shoddily done job.

The distance to the next milepost depends on the mud in the road.
☺Note: The US has 4.09 million miles of road, about 2.65 million miles are paved.

Thirty years one summer.
☺Meaning: A summer that seemed to never end.

Time to go lay the ole frame down.
☺Meaning: Time for bed.

Until the cows come home.
☺Note: Of Scottish origin, from the fact that cows were put out in the spring and would find their way back when scarcity of food forced them home in the fall.

We're burning sunlight.
☺Note: "We're Burning Daylight" - made famous by John Wayne in "The Cowboys."

We're trading daylight for dark.
☺Meaning: We are wasting time.

Whenever I start wishing my life away.
☺Note: One answer to: "When am I getting a pony?"

You can't hurry up good times by waiting for them.
☺"Things may come to those who wait, but only the things left by those who hustle." Abraham Lincoln

You took as long as a month of Sundays.
☺Note: In the 1800's, all sorts of entertainments were prohibited on "Sunday", making the day seem long indeed.

Tough: He's scared of nothing but spiders and dry counties

Toughest individuals I'm aware of are at St. Jude Children's Hospital. They have completely changed how doctors treat children with cancer and other catastrophic illnesses. Since St. Jude was established, the survival rate for acute lymphoblastic leukemia, the most common type of childhood cancer, has increased from 4 percent in 1964 to 94 percent today. During this time, the overall survival rate for childhood cancers has risen from 20 percent to 80 percent. St. Jude has treated children from across the United States and from more than 70 countries.

Please consider St. Jude Children's Hospital in your philanthropy. Here are the sayings you might need to describe those kids.

A snake wouldn't bite him without dying.
☺Note: Copperheads account for more cases of venomous snake bite than any other North American species; however, their venom is the least toxic so their bite is seldom fatal.

Could chew up nails and spit out a barbed wire fence.
☺Rather than: Chuck Norris has already been to Mars; that's why there are no signs of life.

Could go bear hunting with a switch.
☺Note: In 2011, two Canadians died instantly when a car hit a 440-pound black bear, and sent the animal flying straight through the windshield of their vehicle.

He whips his own ass twice a week.
☺Rather than: What is tougher than a Pit-bull with AIDS? ....The guy who gave it to him.

He's the toughest bastard who ever shit behind shoe leather.
☺Note: Apparently one cannot mount a toilet backwards.

He'd shoot craps with the devil himself.
☺Note: If you hear someone say, "The devil jumped up," then you know a shooter "seven-ed out".

He's double backboned
☺"When the going gets tough, the tough get going." Paul 'Bear' Bryant

He's got more guts than you could hang on a fence.
☺Rather than: Chuck Norris doesn't flush the toilet, he scares the shit out of it

He's scared of nothing but spiders and dry counties.
☺Note: Most counties of TX, NE, TN, MI, PA and OH are dry.

He's the only Hell his mama ever raised.
☺"The Bears are so tough when they finish sacking the quarterback, they go after his family in the stands." Tim Wrightman

Like a two dollar steak.
☺Rather than: He's as tough as a boot.

Mean as the alligator when the pond went dry.
☺Rather than: Tough as a pine knot in a sawmill.

Meaner than a skillet full of rattlesnakes.
☺Rather than: If you spell Chuck Norris in Scrabble, you win. Forever.

She raised Hell and stuck a chunk under it.
☺Rather than: Tougher than a one-eared alley cat.

She would charge Hell with a bucket of ice water.
☺Rather than: Make it too tough for the enemy to get in and you can't get out.

Tough as nails and twice as sharp.
☺"Rugby: It is the best sport in the world; it's got everything – speed and tough, ugly men."   Terry O'Connor

Tough as stewed skunk.
☺Rather than: Death once had a near-Chuck Norris experience.

Tough as whitleather.
☺Note: "Whitleather" is animal hide that has been tanned and treated with alum and salt. This process lightens the hide and makes it very durable.

Tougher than a one eared alley cat.
☺Rather than: Chuck Norris doesn't call the wrong number. You answer the wrong phone.

Trifling: It's like two mules fighting over a turnip.

During one of popular culture's most ironic moments, the makers of Trivial Pursuit were accused of "dumbing down" their questions. Was this evidence of the educational system success or failure? Not sure myself, but if you find yourself embroiled in trivial matters, here is how you may respond.

I don't have a dog in that fight.
☺Note: Worldwide, several countries have banned dog fighting, but it is still legal in some countries like Japan, Honduras, and parts of Russia.

I wasn't sitting on the bedpost.
☺Meaning: I wasn't there, so I don't know.

It's like two mules fighting over a turnip.
☺Also: Like trying to see how many butter-beans you can pack up your nose.

Like fleas arguing about who owns the dog.
☺Note: Used famously in "Crocodile Dundee" to describe why the aboriginal people didn't claim to own the land.

Six of one - half dozen of another.
☺Meaning: No difference.

That ain't worth the powder to blow it to Hell.
☺Also: It ain't worth a plug nickel.

Troublesome: Harder to catch than my wife's boyfriend.

In 2012, one of the International Space Stations power distributors broke down. Armed with the most expensive technology available, the astronauts headed outside to replace it. However, metal shavings had built up around the bolts of the old unit, making it impossible to remove with any of the tools NASA had sent. Without a proper tool to remove the shavings the systems, and astronauts, were toast.

- "If only we had a synchronous single-phase PM rotor trapezoidal stator winding besom!" one astronaut said.

- "You mean like a toothbrush?" another responded.

- "No, idiot! Something lightweight with small bristles!"

- "So ... a toothbrush."

The astronauts cleared away the metal shavings using a toothbrush. Once the bolts were clear, they were able to replace the broken unit and restore full power to the station. Whenever you face a problem, remember than simple solutions are often the best.

A tough row to hoe.
☺"There is no success without hardship."   Sophocles

About as hard as trying to herd chickens.
☺ Like tryin to herd cats.

Between a rock and a hard place.
☺"Every cloud has its silver lining but it is sometimes a little difficult to get it to the mint."   Don Marquis

Easy as pissing up a rope.
☺"Putts get real difficult the day they hand out the money."   Lee

Trevino

Harder to catch than my wife's boyfriend.
☺"Being a woman is a terribly difficult task since it consists principally in dealing with men." Joseph Conrad

He'd complain if he was hung from a new rope.
☺"It is never difficult to distinguish between a Scotsman with a grievance and ray of sunshine." P.G. Wodehouse

I'm a stuck duck in a dry pond.
☺Rather than: The ship of state has a difficult road ahead.

I'm going to see to it that it happens, even if it harelips the governor.
☺"The impossible often has a kind of integrity which the merely improbable lacks." Douglas Adams

I'm gonna get it done if it harelips every cow in Texas. (Governor, Pope or President)
☺"In any world menu, Canada must be considered the vichyssoise of nations – it's cold, half-French, and difficult to stir." J. Stuart Keate

It has me by the short and curlies.
☺"What makes resisting temptation difficult for many people is they don't want to discourage it completely." Franklin Jones

It's harder than trying to stick a wet noodle in a wildcat's ass.
☺It is always wise to look ahead, but difficult to look further than you can see." Winston Churchill

Like putting socks on a rooster.
☺"They say being a hostage is difficult… but I could do that with my hands tied behind my back." Phil Nichol

Like snatching shit from a flying goose.
☺"A bird in the hand makes blowing your nose difficult." Solomon

Short

Like trying to bag flies.
☺It is not as difficult as I thought it was, but it is harder than it is.
Eugene Ormandy

Like trying to catch a cat in a whirlwind.
☺"There seems to be some perverse human characteristic that likes to make easy things difficult." Warren Buffett

Like trying to herd cats.
☺"The pollen count, now that's a difficult job… especially if you've got hay fever." Milton Jones

Like trying to nail Jell-O to a tree.
☺"A writer is a person for whom writing is more difficult than it is for other people." Thomas Mann

Like trying to poke a cat out from under the porch with a rope.
☺"There is no movement in the golf swing so difficult that it cannot be made even more difficult by careful study and diligent practice."
Thomas Mulligan

Like trying to shove butter up a wildcat's ass with hot poker.
☺Also: Like licking honey off a blackberry vine

Like trying to stack BB's with a catcher's mitt.
☺"One of the most difficult things in the world is to convince a woman that even a bargain costs money." Edgar Watson Howe

Like washing a cat.
☺Also: Harder than baptizing a cat.

So heavy it'd take three men and a midget to lift it.
☺Rather than: If it looks easy, it's tough… if it looks tough, it's near impossible.

<u>That will separate the sheep from the goats.</u>
☺Meaning: In the last judgment, people are separated by who they follow.

Villains: More slippery than a pocketful of pudding.

For Southerners, nothing says villain like "carpetbagger", a term used to describe outsiders who moved to the South during Reconstruction in order to profit from the instability of the time. "Carpet bag" is the type of luggage which many of these newcomers carried. The term came to be associated with opportunism and exploitation by outsiders and is still used to refer to an outsider perceived as using manipulation or fraud to obtain an objective. Here are the sayings you are likely to come across.

Couldn't fall asleep in a roundhouse.
☺Note: Very few roundhouses remain in use because modern diesel electric locomotives can run equally well in either direction, and many are push-pull trains with control cabs at each end.

Crooked as a barrel full of fish hooks.
☺Fact: Most brands of lipstick contain fish scales.

Crooked as a dog's hind leg.
☺"We hang the petty thieves and appoint the great ones to public office." Aesop's fables.

Crooked as the Brazos.
☺"Wickedness is always easier than virtue; for it takes the short cut to everything." Samuel Johnson

Full of shit as a Christmas turkey.
☺"The main reason Santa is so jolly is because he knows where all the bad girls live." George Carlin

Going to blow the gates of Hell wide open when he goes.
☺"The function of vice is to keep virtue within reasonable bounds." Samuel Butler

He could hide behind a corkscrew.
☺"I am the common denominator to all my bad relationships."
Mike DeStefano

He knows more ways to take your money than a roomful of lawyers.
☺"Our great democracies still tend to think that a stupid man is more likely to be honest than a clever man, and our politicians take advantage of this prejudice by pretending to be even more stupid than nature made them." Bertrand Russell

He runs with the fox and barks with the hounds.
☺Meaning: He'll switch sides depending on who is winning.

He wouldn't know the truth if it slapped him in the face.
☺"I am a politician which means I am a liar and a crook. When I am not kissing babies I am stealing their lollipops." Tom Clancy

He's already got one paw in the chicken coop.
☺Rather than: Pure as the driven slush.

He's lower than a snake fart.
☺Note: Snakes don't pass gas, but they often will defecate and urinate in an attempt to scare predators off. Some snakes also have developed scent glands for defense.

He'd steal the bridle off a night-mare.
☺"The moral world has no particular objection to vice, but an insuperable repugnance to hearing vice called by its proper name."
William Thackeray

He'll put you on the hog train.
☺Note: The "hog train" goes to the bacon factory.

He's on a first-name basis with the bottom of the deck.
☺Note: From a professional poker player: "Chances are you will never catch a professional cheat. Not only will you never catch one, you'll never even suspect one."

He's slicker than a boiled onion.
☺"The great enemy of the truth is very often not the lie, deliberate, contrived and dishonest, but the myth, persistent, persuasive and unrealistic." John F. Kennedy

He's trying to cut a fat hog.
☺Meaning: To take on more than one is able to accomplish.

I would not trust him in a shit house with a muzzle.
☺He would steal the shit-ball from a blind tumble-bug, give him a marble and put him on the wrong road home.

I wouldn't trust him any farther than I can throw him.
☺A half-truth is a whole lie. Yiddish Proverb

Meaner than a sack full of rattlesnakes.
☺He's as crooked as a barrel of snakes.

More twists than a pretzel factory.
☺"If you tell the truth you don't have to remember anything." Mark Twain

Narrow between the eyes.
☺"A lie has speed, but truth has endurance." Edgar J. Mohn

One of them will lie and the other one will swear to it.
☺"The best years are the forties; after fifty a man begins to deteriorate, but in the forties he is at the maximum of his villainy." H.L. Mencken

She's more slippery than a pocketful of pudding.
☺"Corrupt politicians make the other ten percent look bad." Henry Kissinger

Slicker than a slop jar.
☺"It takes two to lie. One to lie and one to listen." Homer Simpson

Slicker than greased owl shit.
☺Always tell the truth. Even if you have to make it up.

So crooked he has to unscrew his britches at night.
☺Rather than: With lies you may get ahead in the world — but you can never go back.   Russian proverb.

So crooked that if he swallowed a nail he'd spit up a corkscrew.
☺"Don't be afraid of enemies who attack you. Be afraid of the friends who flatter you." Dale Carnegie

So crooked you can't tell from his tracks if he's coming or going.
☺"No man has a good enough memory to make a successful liar." Abraham Lincoln

Sooner climb a tree to tell a lie than stand on the ground and tell the truth.
☺Rather than: They would lie if the truth was easier.

Talks out of both sides of his mouth.
☺"Every lie is two lies — the lie we tell others and the lie we tell ourselves to justify it." Robert Brault

The hawk got a job in the chicken yard keeping away the minks.
☺"The least initial deviation from the truth is multiplied later a thousand fold." Aristotle

There are a lot of nooses in his family tree.
☺"The cruelest lies are often told in silence." Adlai Stevenson

Warped like a dogs hind leg.
☺"I don't mind lying, but I hate inaccuracy." Samuel Butler

Well they deserve a front seat in Hell for that.
☺"A lie gets halfway around the world before the truth has a chance to put its pants on." Winston Churchill

<u>Well, they deserve a front seat in Hell for that.</u>
☺"It's the good girls who keep diaries; the bad girls never have the time." Tallulah Bankhead

<u>You can't polish a turd.</u>
☺"Honesty is the first chapter of the book of wisdom." Thomas Jefferson

Wealthy: Shitting in tall cotton.

Southerners generally talk poor even if they aren't. The term "nouveau riche" is reversed for those who flaunt it, no matter how long they have had it. Old money in the South is really old. How about Vanderbilt, Morgan, and Rockefeller? Not old enough.

One never discusses their own wealth, here are the Southern phrases to use to describe others peoples fortune.

Got enough money to burn a wet mule.
☺Note: Mules don't burn easily. Wet mules are even less flammable. If you have enough money to that you could set a wet mule on fire, you have quite a lot.

He buys a new boat when he gets the other one wet.
☺Rather than: He buys a new car when the ashtray is dirty.

He's richer than ten inches up a mule's butt.
☺Note: It's rich alright. Mule (and donkey) manure must be treated carefully so it doesn't burn your plants.

Living high on the hog.
☺Note: The phrase is derived from the fact that the best cuts of meat come from the back and upper leg or 'high on the hog', while the paupers ate belly pork which was low on the hog..

Richer than Croesus.
☺Note: Croesus was the legendary King of Lydia.

Shitting in high cotton.
☺Rather than: Walking in high cotton. Note: The higher the cotton, the better the yield.

Stiff in the heals.

☺Rather than: Well healed.

Walkin' in tall cotton since Napoleon was in knee pants.
☺Note: Until World War I, in many English countries, boys customarily wore short pants in summer.

Yankee rich.
☺Meaning: Really rich.

Weary: Still kickin', but not high, still floppin', but can't fly.

I would like to point out that "South" doesn't necessarily mean "redneck." A redneck is someone who works for a living. Although, working hard does mean mostly Southern according to US News in "The 10 Hardest Working Cities," seven out of ten are in the South. If you are working in the South, you might be needing these sayings.

I feel like 10 miles of bad road.
☺"Oh, I am very weary, though tears no longer flow; my eyes are tired of weeping, my heart is sick of woe." Anne Bronte

I was born tired and since have suffered a relapse.
☺Rather than: I am sick and tire of being sick and tired.

One wheel down and the axle dragging.
☺"The day I made that statement, about the inventing the Internet, I was tired because I'd been up all night inventing the Camcorder." Al Gore

I feel like I was rode hard and put away wet.
☺Note: You should always let your mount cool off for several minutes before a hose down and brushing. With their permission of course.

Shot at and missed, shit at and hit.
☺"I wish I had an answer to that because I'm tired of answering that question. Yogi Berra

Slightly burned out, but still smokin'.
☺"Hear me, my chiefs! I am tired. My heart is sick and sad. From where the sun now stands, I will fight no more forever." Chief Joseph

Still kickin', but not high, still floppin', but can't fly.

☺Meaning: Just doing okay.

Weather: The Devil's beatin' his wife with a frying pan.

It's not just that the South is still close to the land that the weather is a large source of sayings. With maybe a month of winter, and more wide open spaces, you'll be outside more often. It won't take your first born to get a tee time, but you will need to deal with the 90/90 weather (90 degrees and 90 % humidity. Here are the sayings to know.

Cold as a banker's heart.
☺ Cold as loveless duty done.

Cold as a frog's behind.
☺ Cold as the north side of a January gravestone by moonlight.

Cold as a frosted frog.
☺Note: 45- 35 degrees F. Aquatic frogs such as the leopard frog (Rana pipiens) and American bullfrog (Rana catesbeiana) hibernate by burrowing partially in the mud. At this temperature, any exposed frog parts will be frosted.

Cold as a well digger's butt.
☺Rather than: Cold as charity.

Colder than a mother-in-law's love.
☺Rather than: So cold the snowman is asking to come inside.

Colder than day old penguin shit.
☺Rather than: So cold, we didn't clean the house - we defrosted it!

Cold as a cast iron commode.
☺Note: In England, "commode" is often used for a chair enclosing a chamber pot and used in hospitals and the homes of those with incontinence or limited mobility.

Cold enough to freeze the balls off a pool table.

☺Note: Since the game's inception in the 15th Century, billiard balls have been made from many different materials, such as clay, Bakelite, celluloid, crystallite, ivory, plastic, steel and the earliest form, wood.

Cold enough to freeze the tits off a frog.
☺Note: This is between 15-05 degrees F. This saying is just silly of course; everyone knows that frogs can't nurse while hibernating.

Colder than a mother-in-law's kiss.
☺Note: This is 459.67 degrees F. or Absolute zero degrees. It's the lowest possible temperature as molecules cease to move.

Colder than a penguin's balls.
☺"If it's zero degrees outside today and it's supposed to be twice as cold tomorrow, how cold is it going to be?" Steven Wright

Colder than a well digger's nappy.
☺Note: This is between 35-25 degrees. Any colder than that and the contents of the nappy (or diaper) freeze and remain at 32.

Devil's beatin' his wife with a frying pan.
☺Meaning: It's raining and sunny at the same time.

Hotter than a July firecracker.
☺Note: Fireworks are illegal in: IL, IA, OH, VT, NJ, DE, NY, MA and NJ.

Hot as a depot stove.
☺Rather than: Hot as hay harvest.

Hotter n' Hell's basement on the day of reckoning.
☺Rather than: So hot, birds are using potholders to pull worms out of the ground.

Hotter than a $2 pistol.
☺ A-Rod tested positive for Snapple.

Hotter than a billy goat with a blowtorch.
☺Rather than: It's so hot I saw a squirrel putting suntan oil on his nuts.

Hotter than a June bride.
☺Also: It's hotter than a June bride in a feather bed.

Hotter than a setting hen in a wool basket.
☺Rather than: Jehovah's Witnesses started telemarketing.

Hotter than a three-balled tomcat.
☺Rather than: So hot, the cows are giving evaporated milk.

Hotter than Satan's housecat.
☺Also: It's hotter than two cats fighting in a wool sock.

Hotter than the hinges of Hell.
☺Also: It's hotter than a hoot'n poot!

Hotter than two hamsters farting in a wool sock.
☺Also: It's hotter than two cats fighting in a sock.

Hotter than a tick on a dog's balls.
☺Also: It's hotter than a ginger mill in Hades.

Hotter than a biscuit.
☺Also: It is so hot that catfish are fried when you catch them.

Hotter than Satan's toenails.
☺Rather than: Hitchhikers were holding up pictures of thumbs.

Hotter than a four-peckered billy goat.
☺Also: Hotter that a four-peckered billy goat in a pepper patch.

Hotter than a popcorn fart.
☺Also: It is hotter than a jalapeño's cutchie.

Hotter'n seven Hells.
☺Also: It's hotter than hell's pepper patch.

It sure faired off!
☺Meaning: The weather is clearing.

It's been hotter than a goat's butt in a pepper patch.
☺Also: It's hotter than a pepper in a billy goat's butt.

It's been so long since the last rain I had to blow dust out of the rain gauge.
☺Also: So dry the catfish are carrying canteens.

It's cold enough to freeze the balls off a brass monkey.
☺Note: "Brass monkey" was the code name of a famous undercover spy in WW2.

It's colder than a Polar Bear's toenails.
☺Note: Polar Bear habitat may disappear in 50 years if climate trends remain.

It's colder than a whore's heart out there.
☺Also: Cold as a New England audience.

It's going to be a gully-washer.
☺Note: This term is used throughout the heartland.

It's gonna be a frog-strangler.
☺Also: It's gonna be a: gully-washer, cob-floater, duck-drowner, sod-soaker.

It's hotter than a spanked baby's ass.
☺Note: Sixty-five percent of Americans approve of spanking children, a rate that has been steady since 1990. But just 26 percent say grade-school teachers should be allowed to spank kids at school; 72 percent say it shouldn't be permitted, including eight in 10 parents

of grade-schoolers.

It's pouring down bullfrogs.
☺Note: Rain of flightless creatures and objects has been reported throughout history. Roman naturalist Pliny the Elder documented storms of frogs and fish in the 1st century AD.

It's raining pitchforks and plow-handles.
☺Also: It's raining cats and dogs.

It's so cold I saw a politician with his hands in his own pockets.
☺Note: This saying was first heard in 1945 on the radio show of Bob Burns (1890-1956), who was talking about the U.S. Treasury Secretary and "New Dealer," Henry Morganthau.

It's so hot out here I'm getting swamp ass.
☺Meaning: Go and get a pair of new drawers.

It's colder than a brass toilet seat on the shady side of an iceberg.
☺Note: About 5 to −5 degrees F. This range is the interior temperature of the largest recorded iceberg, which incidentally, was 551ft above the surface making it almost a mile deep.

It's colder than a witch's titty in a brass bra doing push-ups in the snow.
☺Note: Cassandra Peterson portrays the horror hostess character Elvira, Mistress of the Dark. Not a witch, but a nice mental picture for the men out there.

It's coming up a bad cloud.
☺Meaning: It looks like rain. Also: It looks like it's going to clabber up and squirt.

It's drier than a popcorn fart.
☺Note: A popcorn fart is dry and non-odoriferous.

It's gonna be a frog choker.

☺Meaning: Wake the kids and call the neighbors.

It's hotter than a hundred acres of burning stumps.
☺Fact: It took 10-15 years for a family of settlers to clear 100 acres of land.

It's hotter than Georgia asphalt.
☺Note: Quoted in the film, "Wild at Heart"

It's hotter than Hell and half of Georgia.
☺Note: Georgia isn't hotter than the rest of the South, but "g" sounds are the next funniest to "k", and Kentucky isn't south enough

It's hotter than the Devil's armpit.
☺Also: Hotter than the Devil's crotch.

It's raining like a crippled cow peeing on a flat rock.
☺Note: Also "Bull on a flat rock. "Words with the hard "k" sound are funnier. You'll notice this as a contrived condition of countless capers.

It's so dry the trees are bribing the dogs.
☺Also: So dry the trees are whistling for the dogs.

It's so hot you could sweat 150 pounds of fat off a 75-pound hog.
☺Note: A "butcher hog", is a pig of approximately 220 lb., is ready for the market.

It's wipe your ass with a snow-cone hot.
☺Note: Quick history of "snow cones." In the 1850s, ice houses in New York would transport the ice to the South in ice wagons. The wagons all passed through Baltimore. Children began asking the waggoneers for a small scraping of ice. Before long, mothers were making flavorings for the ice shavings,

Looks like it's going to clapper up and squirt.
☺Also: Looks like it's coming up a cloud.

Raining so hard the animals are starting to pair up.
☺"It is best to read the weather forecast before we pray for rain."
Mark Twain

So cold we got dogs stuck to fire hydrants all over town.
☺Note: Warm water actually freezes faster than cold because the extra heat energy escapes as steam – that is if the water is allowed to stream out.

So dry the trees are whistling for the dogs.
☺Also: So dry the trees are chasing the dogs.

So foggy, the birds are walking.
☺Note: Birds usually hunker down in the fog, due to decreased sight and sound.

So hot hens are laying hard-boiled eggs.
☺Note: For prefect Hard boiled eggs: Place your raw eggs in a saucepan and cover with 2 inches of cold water and a 1 tablespoon of salt added. High heat until water boils.
Turn off heat, cover and let it sit for 13 minutes.

The bottom is about to fall out.
☺Note: Although rare, a cloudburst can dump over 70,000 tons of water over a square acre.

Yes: Good Lord willing and the creek don't rise.

The Modern English word "yes" comes from the Old English word "gēse", meaning "may it be so." The old way seems far more interesting in a genie sort of way. Viggo Mortensen said, "There's no excuse to be bored. Sad, yes. Angry, yes. Depressed, yes. Crazy, yes. But there's no excuse for boredom, ever." There is not excuse to be boring in the South, use these phrases in good health.

Darn tootin'!
☺Note: Since the early 16th century, "toot" has also meant "to proclaim loudly," "Darn tootin" been used in the US since the 1930s.

Does a bear shit in the woods?
☺Rather than: Does the train stop in the woods to let the lumber jack off?

Does a fat baby fart?
☺Rather than: Does a hobby horse have a pine peter?

Does a one legged duck swim in a circle?
☺Rather than: Does the pope wear a funny hat?

Does a sack of flour make a mighty big biscuit?
☺Also: Does Dolly Parton sleep on her back?

Good Lord willing and the creek don't rise.
☺Also: I'd be tickled.

I could sit still for that.
☺Meaning: An emphatic "Yes!"

I smell what you're stepping in.
☺Rather than: I get a whiff of what you're sitting on.

I'd be tickled pink.
☺Note: The meaning of "tickling" as describing pleasure dates back to the early 1600s.

If that ain't a fact, God's a possum.
☺Meaning: It's true.

If that ain't right then grits ain't groceries.
☺Rather than: Do things mix up have dyslexics?

If you ask kindly, I might could.
☺Meaning: Say the word "please" and I might do it.

Is a frog's ass watertight?
☺Rather than: Is a pig's ass pork?

Is a ten pound robin fat?
☺Rather than: Can you teach a rock to stay?

Might as well. Can't dance, never could sing, and it's too wet to plow.
☺Meaning: I might as well.

Plumb tickled to death.
☺Meaning: Thank you for asking, I'd be tickled, i.e. very pleased.

Sho 'nuff!
☺Meaning: Of course!

Straight from the horse's mouth.
☺Note: In racing, the most trusted authorities are those closest in touch: stable lads, trainers etc. From the horse's mouth' is supposed to indicate one step better, that is, the horse itself.

Sure as a cat's got climbing gear.
☺Rather than: Does Raggedy Ann have cotton tits?

That dog will hunt.
☺Also: That cat will wash.

You can't beat that with a stick.
☺Also: You can't lick that with a Weedwacker.

You're not just whistling Dixie!
☺Note: "Dixie" was Abe Lincoln favorite tune, and was often played by Union bands.

Your druthers are my ruthers.
☺Meaning: We Agree.

Prologue

Southerners often argue over who is "Southern." This is an excellent indication that being Southern is something to aspire to. What then defines being Southern and who can be one? The answer is anyone. If you enjoyed this book and put these sayings to work - you're as Southern as Dixie. I hope you enjoy this book and the culture of the South.

About the Author

Tim Heaton is from Southaven Mississippi and is an Ole Miss Alumnus. After a 25 year career on Wall Street, the markets decided he was a better writer than trader. He writes on history, technology and finance. He has lived in Santa Monica, Chicago, Memphis, Atlanta, Baltimore, New York and London England. Today, Tim lives in Morristown NJ where he is currently annoying his friends and family with tall tales from Dixie.

34509549R00124

Made in the USA
San Bernardino, CA
30 May 2016